Praise for *The Mindful Teacher's*

This is an easy-to-follow, practical and useful handbook for busy teachers, written by someone who clearly understands both mindfulness and the pressures of the classroom and staffroom. It provides a clear and approachable introduction to mindfulness theory and practice which is enough to help a 'beginner' get going and enticing enough to lead on those who take to it (and not all teachers will, of course) into further practice and study. What is particularly novel and helpful is the application of mindfulness practice to the everyday and potentially difficult experiences all teachers will know well, such as transitions, the dreaded inspections and meeting with challenging parents and colleagues.

Katherine Weare, Emeritus Professor, University of Southampton, Lead for Education for the Mindfulness Initiative and author, with Zen Master Thich Nhat Hahn, of the bestseller *Happy Teachers Change the World*

The work of teaching our young people is one of the most important and impactful jobs to engage in. It is also challenging, stressful and time squeezed. How can teachers look after themselves, remain creative and keep in touch with their love for their vocation in the midst of these pressures? Get this book and allow it to be an ongoing companion to your journey. Keep revisiting the pages. It offers rich resources supporting you to keep your mindfulness practice going and creatively adapt it to you and your life. It also gives you very practical ideas, tailored to the school teaching context, on how to realise the fruits of your mindfulness practice in everyday life – both during routine and high-stress times. If you are a schoolteacher, this book has your back.

Professor Rebecca Crane, PhD, Director, Centre for Mindfulness Research and Practice, Bangor University

We all know how stressful it can be working in the education sector. This is a practical book full of great ideas and written by an author who understands the pressures faced by educationalists. Thoroughly recommend.

Simon Pirotte, OBE, Principal and CEO, Bridgend College

As the well-being imperative in schools and colleges grows ever more urgent, *The Mindful Teacher's Handbook* has to be a go-to resource for anyone in education who wants to thrive in their role and take meaningful well-being practice in schools to a new and necessary level. Kamalagita acts as our guide as she thoughtfully explores and connects the science, practice and benefits of mindfulness, sharing clear strategies and exercises that are both teacher-friendly and supported by engaging discussions.

Natalie Chyba, Deputy Principal and Well-Being Lead, Howell's School, Llandaff

Kamalagita's vast experience as a mindfulness trainer, teacher of young people and collaborator with schools on their mindfulness journey means that she is in a unique position to write this accessible guide to a more spacious life.

Whether you are new to teaching, a hardened professional with many years of experience, a classroom assistant or a senior leader, this book has something for you. Kamalagita gives us permission to recognise that we are all human and that we share many more of our common day-to-day experiences than we might like to think.

Jane Barnes, Deputy Head Teacher, Teaching and Learning and CPD, Manchester

What an uplifting read. *The Mindful Teacher's Handbook* is exactly what every teacher needs to have within arm's reach at all times. It's easily accessible, taking you through a series of mindfulness exercises which gradually become habit-forming. Since reading the book, I've found myself constantly (sometimes unconsciously) going through some of the exercises and enjoying the positive impact mindfulness can have.

Armando Di-Finizio, retired Head Teacher, educational consultant
and author of *A Head Full of Ethos*

The Mindful Teacher's Handbook is a book for every teacher and leader in an ever-changing world. The book is well timed, as we begin our new curriculum journey in Wales, with a real focus on how we all need to focus on our own health and well-being: we can only care for our students with empathy and love if we 'mind our own minds'. There is nothing 'woolly' about this book; it is written with authenticity and is rooted in classroom experience. The section on using mindfulness as a tool for responding to some of the behaviours we are all seeing in the post-COVID-19 classroom is both refreshing and useful.

Overall, there is a toughness about this writing: an insistence on the absolute need to build in mindfulness that I found compelling and very real. I see a need for this handbook in my school and in every school.

Jennifer Ford, Head Teacher, Treorchy Comprehensive School

I really like this book. What I like about it is that it's realistic and useful. Kamalagita has written accessibly for the busy teacher-reader and it is full of exercises and systems that support a more mindful approach to the day-to-day stresses of school life. It'll help teachers rediscover the joy in what they do.

Hywel Roberts, teacher, writer, humourist, author of
Botheredness: Stories, Stance and Pedagogy

Absolutely delighted to review this informative, evidence-based and helpful handbook from Kalamagita Hughes. Harnessing the principles of a whole school approach to emotional well-being using person-centred approaches, this book is much needed at a time when COVID-19 has exacerbated concerns about children and young people's mental health and the role of community action. The strategies to promote well-being in our communities will be fundamental to tackling this issue and Kalamagita portrays this beautifully in structured and easy-to-read instructions. The reader will be able to understand the biological reasons, practise and evaluate the outcomes of their interventions and ensure the whole school community benefits from emotional regulation in the promotion of relationships and well-being. A much-needed resource!

Ceri Reed, Director of Parents Voices in Wales CIC

As an educationalist, if you were in two minds about whether mindfulness is for you, fear not. This book is crammed with some fabulous exercises that will help you find peace, balance and a new sense of energy and focus. It's an easy-to-read, well-planned book which guides you effortlessly through the why, what and how of mindfulness implementation. I thoroughly enjoyed reading and practising many of the techniques. Thank you, Kamalagita, for a lovely magical mindfulness handbook for teachers.

Nina Jackson, International Mental Health and Well-Being Advisor, Teach Learn Create Ltd

If you've ever wondered if mindfulness might have something to offer your own well-being or that of your pupils, this comprehensive but accessible book will guide you to a decision. As a busy teacher you'll appreciate the clear and succinct descriptions of mindfulness, how it can help and why it works, set directly in the context of school/college settings and relevant situations. It's written for teachers by a teacher whose classroom experience shows through on every page.

Elizabeth Williams, mindfulness teacher and Chair and Education Lead for Mindfulness Wales CIO

Thank you for such a great book for educational professionals. It is certainly a must-read. The book provides a clear insight into mindfulness, starting with its background and how mindfulness can be applied within the educational setting. The practical tips are easily applied to activities within the classroom, especially to self-regulate – for both staff and students! With health and well-being becoming a focus within the new curriculum, this book is a must for all teachers.

Luisa Martin Thomas, Deputy Head Teacher, Cyfarthfa High School, Pearson UK Teacher of the Year 2017–2018, mindfulness advocate

There is widespread concern about the mental well-being of children and young people. Teachers are such an important influence on their lives. With so many teachers experiencing stress themselves, it is all the more important to have practical ideas to help. This is an excellent introduction to mindfulness, offering many practical exercises to help teachers manage the 'internal weather' that daily events frequently stir up. When people feel less stressed, less at risk of burnout and more focused on the purpose that brought them into teaching in the first place, it is also a valuable help for all the children they teach and influence. The testimonies of the people who have benefitted are woven through this straightforward and practical guide.

Jenny Edwards, CBE, Health Advisor, Mindfulness Initiative

This is an opportunity for educators to learn more about mindfulness, whether they practise regularly or are new to the field. This book's welcoming atmosphere offers a wealth of information and explains mindfulness in a clear, simple and factual way. The author's education background ensures that this resource is not only relevant but useful, with specific examples for the busy periods of the academic year. Many case studies are included from all areas of education which ensures that users are able to make the most of an activity or idea from the outset. A useful resource to use in the world of education for years to come – thank you, Kamalagita.

Nia Brodrick, Mental Health Project Officer (2018–2019), ColegauCymru

This is a superb toolkit for all staff whether you are new to the profession, an experienced teacher or member of the school leadership team. What I love about the book is that regardless of your perceptions or thoughts about mindfulness, there is such a strong focus on well-being and responding (not reacting!) to the busy school lives that we all lead. The layout is very easy to navigate, and each chapter has excellent activities that are so simple to implement without a huge amount of preparation. Highly recommend this as a book of choice for anyone working in a school environment. I will definitely be dipping in and sharing with colleagues – wonderful to have all this rich material at our fingertips!

Shirley Drummond, Head Teacher, St Helen's College

Kamalagita Hughes

The Mindful Teacher's Handbook

How to step out of busyness and find peace

Crown House Publishing Limited

www.crownhouse.co.uk

First published by
Crown House Publishing Limited
Crown Buildings, Bancyfelin, Carmarthen, Wales, SA33 5ND, UK
www.crownhouse.co.uk
and
Crown House Publishing Company LLC
PO Box 2223, Williston, VT 05495, USA
www.crownhousepublishing.com

First published 2022.

p. 37, figure: *The Compassionate Mind*. © Paul Gilbert, 2010. Reproduced with permission of the licensor through PLSclear.
p. 50, figure: The Exhaustion Funnel. © Marie Åsberg from www.mindfulnext.org/
p. 68, poem: The Guest House © C. Barks, from The *Essential Rumi* (New York: HarperCollins, 1995).
p. 121, poem: The Goose in the Bottle © L. France, from The *Heart as Origami* (London: Parallax Press, 2005).

British Library Cataloguing-in-Publication Data
A catalogue entry for this book is available from the British Library.

Print ISBN 978-178583642-8
Mobi ISBN 978-178583644-2
ePub ISBN 978-178583645-9
ePDF ISBN 978-178583646-6
LCCN 2022935937

Printed and bound in the UK by
Charlesworth Press, Wakefield, West Yorkshire

For Susan and Meurig Hughes,
the best teachers I ever knew.

Acknowledgements

I would like to thank all the teachers, heads and teaching assistants that I have taught over the last eight years; your commitment to your vocation and compassion for those you care for has inspired me. Heartfelt thanks to those of you who were generous enough to share your stories on how mindfulness has impacted on your teaching life; these have formed the backbone of this book.

Thanks to Stella Gunningham for her wonderful illustrations that illuminate the book. I am deeply grateful that you found the time to create these on top of a full-time teaching job and busy family life.

Many thanks to David, Karen and Beverley at Crown House Publishing, for giving me the opportunity. Particular thanks to my editors Daniel and Ting who made the writing of the book a smooth and straightforward process.

Thanks to my colleague Sofia Pereira, for allowing me to drop everything in the last week and focus on the book – I knew things would be in safe hands. Last but not least, thanks to my husband, Vishvapani Blomfield, who not only steadied me when I doubted but gave his practical knowledge of writing, editing and publishing. To my son, Leo, for understanding when Mum was busier than usual. And to my dog, Tessa, who kept me walking and sifting the ideas.

Contents

Acknowledgements .... *i*

An Introduction to Mindfulness: Ancient Wisdom Supported by Modern Science 1

Brief history of secular mindfulness 2

Why education? 4

How can mindfulness help school staff? 6

Putting on the oxygen mask first 7

Excuses that crop up 8

A word of caution 9

How to use this book 10

Mindfulness with an attitude 11

How to use the mindfulness exercises 11

School communities and case studies 12

This is a handbook 12

Chapter 1: Creating the Weather in the Classroom 13

Finding Calm 13

Centring the weather vane 13

Tuning in 15

What did you notice? 15

Why this matters 16

Coming to your senses 17

What did you notice? 18

Why this matters: autopilot and mindfulness 19

Stepping out of autopilot 21

Emotional barometer 21

Finger breathing – a tool to calm 23

Chapter 2: Breaking Up Is Never Easy 25

The Art of Making Transitions in the School Day 25

Why this matters: from doing to being mode 27

The mindful minute 29

Stepping out of autopilot: the routine activity 31

What did you notice? 31

Why this matters 32

Chapter 3: Behaviour Management 35

Responding, not Reacting 35

Awareness of self 36

Awareness of other 37

Awareness of environment 41

Awareness of the bigger picture 42

Mindfulness exercises to try 43

What did you notice? 44

Why does this matter? 44

Playful body scan 45

What did you notice? 47

Why does this matter? 48

Chapter 4: Mindfulness for Stressful Times 49

For an Inspection 49

Before the inspection 50

Before inspection 52

During the inspection 53

After the inspection 55

Mindfulness exercises to try 55

Mile track practice 56

Mindful movement sequence 57

Gentle stretching (can be done in a chair too) 60

Opening to the sky and earth (can be done in a chair or standing) 61

Mindful walking 62

What did you notice? 62

Why does this matter? 63

Chapter 5: Working with Thoughts and Overthinking 65

The Guest House 68

Thoughts are not facts 69

Mindfulness exercises to try 69

Why this matters 71

Meditation: approaching rather than avoiding 72

What did you notice? 73

Why does this matter? 74

Chapter 6: Mindfulness for Stressful Times **75**

For an Observation 75

Mindfulness exercise to try 77

What did you notice? 78

Why is this important? 78

The mind: like Velcro for bad experiences and Teflon for good ones 79

Mindfulness in decision-making 79

Mindfulness exercise to try 80

What did you notice? 81

Why this matters 81

Surviving and thriving in an observation/learning walk/work scrutiny 82

Grounding practice 83

What did you notice? 84

After the observation/learning walk/work scrutiny 85

Why this matters 85

Chapter 7: Mindfulness for Stressful Times **87**

Difficult Communication with a Colleague/Manager or Parent 87

Mindfulness exercises to try 92

50–50 awareness 92

What did you notice? 93

Why this matters 94

What did you notice? 95

Why this matters 95

Chapter 8: Filling the Tank **97**

Kindness and Self-Compassion 97

Self-care is not selfish 99

Regal walking 100

Facial expression 101

Self-talk and voice tone 102

What did you notice practising these three exercises? 102

Why this matters 103

You deserve kindness 103

Friendliness meditation 104

What did you notice? 106

Why does this matter? 107

Chapter 9: Mindfulness and Creativity in the Classroom **109**

An example of creativity in the classroom: Supported Learning Experiments 110

Creating a mindful setting 112

Convergent and divergent thinking 114

Mindfulness exercises to try 115

Habit releasers 115

What did you notice? 117

Why does this matter? 118

The nine dots exercise 118

What do you notice? 119

Wobbling and staying still 119

What did you notice? 120

Why this matters 121

The Goose and the Bottle 121

Chapter 10: Under Pressure **123**

From Surviving to Thriving 123

Exercise: Exploring feelings of stress in the body and stressful thoughts in the mind 124

Why does this matter? 126

Mindfulness exercises to try 127

From scattered to focused 127

What did you notice? 128

Why this matters 128

Not surviving but thriving 129

Nourishing/depleting activities 129

What did you notice? 130

Why this matters 130

Chapter 11: Becoming a Mindfulness Champion **135**

What does it mean to be a mindfulness champion? 135

Why does this matter? 136

How can you gain the confidence and competence to pass the skills on to others? 137

Why this matters 142

Mindfulness champions: takeaways 143

How can you convince senior leadership that this is what the school/college really needs? 144

Local authority approach 146
Why does this matter? 147
The tortoise approach 148
Mindfulness exercises to try 149
Daring to dream 149
Why this matters 150
Mapping the territory 151
Why this matters 152

Chapter 12: Mindful Ideas to Try in the Classroom **153**
Early years 153
Primary school 154
Secondary school 155
College and post-16 setting 158
Final Thoughts 159

Resources *161*
For your practice 161
Bringing mindfulness into your workplace 163
Mindfulness training for the classroom 163
The evidence base 164

Bibliography *165*

About the author *168*

An Introduction to Mindfulness

Ancient Wisdom Supported by Modern Science

A group of adults sit together in silence in a room.

They are setting themselves up before the start of the day. They are focusing on their breath and, as they do so, they notice that they are feeling calmer and more centred. The spaces between their thoughts become more noticeable, the urges to plan the day or review what's gone on begin to subside. There may be background noise or hubbub, but this doesn't bother them; they know this is par for the course.

Their minds wander off, but they've learnt to notice this and bring them back to the breath. They know that they can settle and recentre themselves again. But they are not in an ashram or a Buddhist temple, they're at work: in school, in a business, in the military or even in prison.

When I started to practise mindfulness meditation 25 years ago, it was still niche, put in a category with yoga, chakra cleansing, something New Age or 'hippy'. At the time, New Labour were campaigning to become the new government, and public perception would probably have identified mindfulness as something more to do with the campaigning Natural Law Party with their yogic flying, a technique where meditators jumped up and down in full lotus position. The public would have shaken their heads in disbelief if anyone had said that, 20 years later, politicians would be practising mindfulness in Parliament.[1]

Mindfulness is not a new practice; it's a human capacity that goes back over 2,500 years. It's a natural capacity that we can all cultivate that has become associated with authentic happiness. Most ancient religions and philosophies have a history of contemplative traditions. However, mindfulness has now exploded into the wider public eye, particularly in the last decade, as mindfulness practices have been combined with modern psychological theories to create secular practices that have been the subject

---

1   Mindful Nation UK report (London: The Mindfulness Initiative, 2015). Available at: https://www.themindfulnessinitiative.org.

of thousands of scientific trials.[2] The scientific element has helped us have a clearer understanding of how our brains work – but, more importantly to us as human beings, it shows us how our *minds* work. It helps us understand the complex jumble of thoughts, feelings, emotions, memories and impulses, moment to moment. It's also shown that we can train our minds to focus, be aware, and cultivate compassion and wise attitude.

Brief history of secular mindfulness

Despite being an ancient contemplative tradition, mindfulness as we recognise it in this form stems from the work of Jon Kabat-Zinn from his time at the University of Massachusetts in 1979. Jon was a child of the 1960s, and like most baby boomers was captivated by the potential for meditations and philosophies from the East to change society. But he was also a research scientist – and therefore when the opportunity came to teach some of these practices in the context of the University of Massachusetts Medical School, he started to collect the data. The first mindfulness course in this mould was provided for people in intense chronic pain or with terminal illnesses. They had been dealt their final card; the doctors had said there was nothing more they could do for their pain or illness. In a bold move, Jon Kabat-Zinn started to teach these participants gentle yoga and mindfulness meditation. While their symptoms didn't go away, the participants realised that the stress, despair and hopelessness that they felt about their condition was layering on more tension and suffering to an already difficult situation. By learning and practising these techniques, they discovered that although the symptoms continued, they could choose to respond to these in a way that didn't add more suffering and tension and therefore free their minds and find some peace.[3] In this way, mindfulness-based stress reduction (MBSR) was born.

In the late 1990s, a team of clinical psychologists went over to visit Jon Kabat-Zinn in the Stress Reduction clinic to observe and train in MBSR delivery. Their research showed that if someone had depression once, then they would be likely to experience it again. Seeing how depression robbed people of their lives, they were keen to find a way of helping people train their minds to handle difficult thoughts and emotions when they were well before another relapse into depression. This team of Mark Williams, John Teasdale and Zindel Segal created mindfulness-based cognitive therapy (MBCT), which

---

2   K. Weare and A. Bethune, *Implementing Mindfulness in Schools: An Evidence-Based Guide* (Sheffield: The Mindfulness Initiative, 2021). Available at: https://www.themindfulnessinitiative. org/implementing-mindfulness-in-schools-an-evidence-based-guide.

3   J. Kabat-Zinn, *Full Catastrophe Living: Using the Wisdom of the Body and Mind to Ease Stress, Pain, and Illness* (New York: Delta, 1990).

has been approved by the National Institute of Clinical Excellence (NICE) in the UK for the prevention of recurrent depression since 2004 and is offered routinely by the NHS. Clinical trials have shown that MBCT is at least as effective for treating clinical depression and anxiety as taking anti-depressants.[4]

These are the two main roots from which most secular mindfulness programmes spring, and there are now hundreds of mindfulness-based programmes out there. In the last decade, cutting-edge employers like Apple and Google have offered mindfulness training to employers to help them manage stress and to thrive, notably Google's programme with the catchy title 'Search Inside Yourself'.[5] But it's not just for the cool kids in Google and Apple.

'Meditate like a Marine for pumped up mental muscle!' is an attention-grabbing headline from an article pointing to the fact that the US Marines have been taught mindfulness to prepare for combat. In deployment, mindfulness is found to help soldiers stay calm during crisis and mitigate the effect of post-traumatic stress disorder.[6]

In the last decade, mindfulness has been taught by the NHS, in schools, in workplaces such as Tata Steel, Jaguar Land Rover and HSBC,[7] and in prisons and probation settings with a small-scale research on impact carried out by the National Offender Management System.[8]

In 2015, the Mindfulness Initiative worked with a cross-party parliamentary group to look at the efficacy and potential impact of mindfulness in the workplace, healthcare, criminal justice and schools. The result was the UK Mindful Nation Report,[9] which was

---

4   There is even newer evidence that mindfulness should be offered as first treatment for newer, less severe depression as well as relapse; see NICE, *Depression in Adults: Treatment and Management*, NICE Guideline [NG222] (London: National Institute for Health and Care Excellence, 2022). Available at: https://www.nice.org.uk/guidance/ng222/chapter/Recommendations#preventing-relapse.

5   D. Penman, *Mindfulness for Creativity: Adapt and Create in a Frantic World* (London: Piatkus, 2015).

6   L. Zerbe, Meditate like a Marine to pump up your mental muscles, *Signs of the Times* (14 March 2009). Available at: https://www.sott.net/article/256955-Meditate-like-a-Marine-to-pump-up-your-mental-muscles.

7   The Mindfulness Initiative, *Building the Case for Mindfulness in the Workplace*. (Sheffield: The Mindfulness Initiative, 2016). Available at: https://www.themindfulnessinitiative.org/Handlers/Download.ashx?IDMF=46ef10fd-4d64-41f9-91a6-163d52cd304c.

8   J. Davies, C. Hurrell, P. Raynor, P. Ugwadike and H. Young, A pragmatic study of the impact of a brief mindfulness intervention on prisoners and staff in a Category B prison and men subject to community-based probation supervision, *International Journal of Offender Therapy and Comparative Criminology* (2020). Available at: https://journals.sagepub.com/doi/full/10.1177/0306624X20944664.

9   See https://www.themindfulnessinitiative.org/mindful-nation-report.

a real game-changer in terms of the public perception of, and willingness to approach, mindfulness.

I am hoping that you are coming to see that mindfulness is not the preserve of woolly headed navel-gazers, as I thought, but of ordinary people like you and me.

Why education?

The links between well-being and education for staff and students have been high up on the agenda of schools and colleges, the inspectorate and policymakers lately. This is because a clear link has been made between young people's well-being and their ability to learn.[10] You will know this from your own experience: if a young person is struggling, has issues at home or school, they can't settle and learn as well as one who has a stable home life or enjoys meaningful friendships at school.

Approximately 25% of young people have a recognisable mental health disorder, with 10% needing specialist help. What's heart-breaking is that 50% of mental health issues are established by the age of 15 and 75% before the age of 25.[11] And three-quarters of young people across the age span do not receive the help they need.[12] Most child and adolescent mental health services are bursting at the seams and cannot cope with the higher demand. This is before we get to low-level anxiety or stress symptoms that can quickly escalate into something more serious if not caught and addressed. The need for taking this seriously is even more pressing in the context of the global COVID-19 pandemic, where many young people have missed out on the stability and structure of school and college, have been isolated from friends and peer groups, and are living in a societal atmosphere of fear and worry. This serious gap in the provision for young people mean that the parents, schools and colleges pay the price.

---

10 Public Health England, *The Link Between Pupil Health and Wellbeing and Attainment: A Briefing for Head Teachers, Governors and Staff in Education Settings* (London: Public Health England, 2014). Available at: https://assets.publishing.service.gov.uk/government/uploads/system/uploads/attachment_data/file/370686/HT_briefing_layoutvFINALvii.pdf.

11 Mental Health Foundation, *Mental Health Statistics: Children and Young People* (London: Mental Health Foundation, 2020). Available at: https://www.mentalhealth.org.uk/explore-mental-health/statistics/children-young-people-statistics.

12 R. C. Kessler, P. Berglund, O. Demler, R. Jin, K. R. Merikangas and E. E. Walters, Lifetime prevalence and age-of-onset distributions of DSM-IV disorders in the national comorbidity survey replication, *Archives of General Psychiatry* 62(6) (2005): 593–602. Available at: https://pubmed.ncbi.nlm.nih.gov/15939837/.

The evidential link between young people practising mindfulness and their well-being is well researched.[13] The results are promising. A summary of benefits are as follows:[14]

- Mindfulness benefits many aspects of psychosocial well-being including positive mood, empathy and connectedness across all ranges.

- It impacts aspects of physical well-being in the young such as blood pressure, heart rate, cortisol and improvement in sleep.

- It helps reduce student mental health problems including burnout, depression and stress with emerging evidence for impacts on anxiety, trauma, eating and sleep disorders.

- It impacts social and emotional skills and self-management including emotional literacy, regulation resilience and relational skills such as sociability.

- Mindfulness impacts on aspects of learning and cognition, executive function, attention and focus, and cognitive flexibility.

- There is a small amount of emerging evidence of impacts on academic performance and results on test of achievement and grade scores.

- There is also a small amount of emerging evidence for impacts on behaviour, such as students with attention deficit hyperactivity disorder.

Mindfulness is a relatively low-cost intervention that can help prevent low-level issues escalating into higher ones. But it also allows young people to thrive, to be at their best and value their talents. In an uncertain future, with issues such as an ecological crisis and the rise of artificial intelligence on the horizon, young people will be inhabiting a very different world to ours. We don't know the content of the future, but giving them the skills of focus, resilience, flexibility and creativity, as well as being able to relate, be emotionally intelligent and empathic, will give them the best chance to them face it.

---

13 Weare and Bethune, *Implementing Mindfulness in Schools*, p. 89.
14 Weare and Bethune, *Implementing Mindfulness in Schools*, p. 32.

How can mindfulness help school staff?

I have just made the case for the benefits that mindfulness can bring to young people. So why is this book for teachers and school and college staff?

Figures from the *Teacher Wellbeing Index*, a current and well-respected document report, states that three-quarters of teachers experience work-related stress, with nearly half reporting depression, anxiety or panic attacks at work. At any one time, more than half are considering leaving the profession due to poor health and figures reported are higher for senior leaders.[15] There is a national teacher shortage, with dropping numbers recruited for initial teacher training, and one in seven of these leave the profession within the first year.[16] We are losing our most experienced teachers, and we can't recruit and sustain new ones. It's a tragedy for the profession and, most of all, for the young people who are so in need of the support, encouragement and care that an effective teacher or teaching assistant (TA) can bring.

You don't need me to tell you this because I imagine that you are experiencing this every day on the front line. If you're reading this, the chances are that you already know that something needs to change, that it is increasingly difficult to keep on going in the ways that the education system is currently demanding.

So here's some good news. Mindfulness-based interventions have been shown to:

▨ Increase teacher/school/college staff well-being including a sense of a purpose, self-care, compassion and physical health.[17]

▨ Help reduce school staff mental health problems, such as burnout, depression, stress and anxiety.

▨ Improve the ability to self-regulate, to pay attention and be more in the moment and find calm.

▨ Help school staff stand back from gripping thoughts and emotions, and respond more flexibly and creatively in the moment.

▨ Allow school staff to be more effective in the classroom, focusing on concepts and processes rather than content and behaviour, and stay on task rather than be taken off track.

---

15 Mental Health Foundation, *Mental Health Statistics*.

16 D. Speck, One in seven NQTs drop out in first year, *TES* (13 September 2019). Available at: https://www.tes.com/news/one-seven-nqts-drop-out-first-year.

17 All that applies to school staff, applies to college staff now, but from now on I will refer to 'school staff' for fluency and ease.

■ Help school staff to relate to students with increased empathy and create calmer and more focused classroom environments.[18]

The most valuable aspect to me was the knowledge of how I could take time to calm myself in a very frantic environment and how simple that was to do.

(Secondary school teacher)

I'm happier, my staff are happier, my pupils are happier!

(Primary school head teacher)

Putting on the oxygen mask first

Anyone who works in a school is in the caring profession – and therefore they are motivated to act by the needs of another. However, for any carer, exhaustion and burnout is a real concern. On an aeroplane, we are told in the safety instructions that in the event of an emergency we should put on our own oxygen mask first and then help the other. The same goes for well-being: we need to look after ourselves in order to give and be a resource for others. It sounds counterintuitive and you may feel guilty or self-indulgent for focusing on yourself. But this tendency of being other-oriented needs balance, as your needs are important too.

My top suggestion? Put staff well-being at the top of the agenda. Start with the adults!

(Lynburn Primary School, Fife[19])

---

18 Weare and Bethune, *Implementing Mindfulness in Schools*, p. 27.
19 Weare and Bethune, *Implementing Mindfulness in Schools*, p. 28.

Excuses that crop up

'I just want to be able help the kids!' Any school staff member will have the young people they care for as top priority. However, to effectively introduce young people to mindfulness, you need some understanding of what mindfulness is (and what it isn't) and some experience of practising it yourself. Put simply, mindfulness is the art of becoming present, truly present, and this takes practice. This is because mindfulness is *caught*, not *taught*. It is a skill, but it needs to be experienced in order to truly appreciate its benefits. An analogy is that you wouldn't teach someone to swim by reading a book out to them from the side of the pool. The same goes for mindfulness.

'I don't have time for this/myself!' I get it! You are already a busy person and here you are needing to find more time. However, most of the practices in this book take between 2 and 20 minutes. There is something to suit everyone. Ask yourself how much you value your own well-being if you cannot take 2 minutes out of the day. Not only that, but think about how much time we waste (I'm including myself here) on so-called relaxing – watching rubbish on the telly that you aren't really interested in, scrolling through social media while trying to do something else. We want to 'switch off' but may find ourselves feeling even more distracted, listless and frustrated. Making a conscious decision to do something nourishing for yourself and putting that time aside can mean that you sleep better, feel more refreshed and energised, and don't burn out.

'What will people think of me?' You may feel a little shy about these exercises and others seeing you at home or in the workplace. But many of the exercises can be done with your eyes open, in informal settings, like walking down a corridor, or sitting in your car before or after work. You have the luxury of keeping this to yourself until you know that it works. Then you can shout it from the rooftops if you wish, although you probably won't have to; people will have noticed a change in you and be asking what you're doing!

'This is flaky mumbo-jumbo!' Trying something new can be daunting, but the solid body of evidence attests to the improvements mindfulness can bring to your life. This is science, not self-indulgence. If thousands of school staff have found this helpful, wouldn't it be worth giving it a go? If you try it and find that it doesn't work for you, that's fine, you can move on. But you will have tried rather than dismissing it out of hand.

A word of caution

The evidence shows that mindfulness can help in addressing the mental health of the school community and stress. Adverse effects are rare but need to be looked out for.[20] However, like anything else, mindfulness is not a magic wand or a silver bullet that will solve all life's problems. And it is in no way being advocated here as a sticking plaster to mask the systemic stress present in the current education system. However, it will give school staff greater awareness of their own feelings and needs and how to address these, thereby empowering them. This will also give them greater clarity and choice in how to address difficulties they experience on a daily basis.

Here are some examples of school staff who have become interested and tried mindfulness:

Lindsey is a TA in a nursery class:

> I had a crisis going on. I needed to find things I could do myself rather than go to the GP for anti-depressants. It was a natural development, I heard a lot about it and was quite interested in the neuroscience behind it. It helped, it gave me a toolkit.

Mike is a primary school teacher:

> It started as a joke between me and my wife; I don't think that multi-tasking is a thing. Teaching is a stressful job and I thought, it's only going to be helpful, so that's what drew me to it.

Belle is an early years teacher:

> For years my husband had been buying me books and telling me that I needed to do this. But it wasn't the right time for me, so then I had the realisation that I could do this now and was amazed how quickly it seemed to make a difference.

Tim is a secondary school teacher:

> I experienced my own stress in life. I thought that I was clear, I trusted my judgements and all of a sudden I didn't trust my judgements. In school there are different demands that come all at once and they're often competing. As a teacher, your priority is the interaction with the kids, but often you're torn, and you end up spending more time on an admin task and then interaction with the kids gets squeezed. That's frustrating. I studied psychology as part of my degree and found the neuroscience element really interesting.

---

20 Weare and Bethune, *Implementing Mindfulness in Schools*, p. 24.

Simon is the head of a primary school:

> I realised that I needed to make time for myself in a professional way which would help me personally as well. I needed some other strategies to help me cope with the pressure. The pressures are more extreme and intense, that's what made me take the plunge because I always felt guilty about taking school time for myself and my role.

Tom is the head of a primary school:

> I was a bit cynical about it as I didn't know enough about it. Speaking to my chair of governors, I thought, 'It's something for me. It'll give me a chance to reflect and learn more about mindfulness and see how it can help me in my role.'

Claire, safeguarding and well-being manager in a college:

> I was quite cynical. I had this stereotypical image of people eating fruit mindfully and thought I haven't got time for that. But then I was intrigued how many people found it useful and positive, so I tried to approach it with an open mind.

Ready to give it go? Let's get started.

How to use this book

This book is suitable for complete beginners to mindfulness. There are enough theory and suggested practices to get you going and bring mindfulness into your life in a meaningful way. However, I was also motivated to write this book because the mindfulness world is largely set up around the 'eight-week course'. While this might be an effective means to train people in mindfulness, it's not in terms of carrying on and sustaining mindfulness practice. You wouldn't take up yoga for eight weeks and then never go to a yoga class again. So this book is also meant to be a resource for those who have already trained in mindfulness but are finding it hard to sustain a practice over time.

The chapters in the book are structured to introduce you in a step-by-step way to mindfulness exercises and how they can benefit you in daily life. Each chapter includes a rationale – a story, theory or explanation – and then some exercises to choose, practise and reflect on. The material has been grouped into themes, which are identified in in-depth interviews with school staff as being the most pressing and pertinent to them. I hope they will speak to you.

Even though the book is structured so that each chapter augments the next, being a teacher I know what we are like! We scan the material to absorb it quickly. There might be something that jumps out at you immediately and you think, 'Yes, I need help with that!' By all means, dive in, but bear in mind that some of the chapters will refer you to previous chapters, in which case it would be wise to go back to these to fill in any gaps.

Mindfulness with an attitude

Although secular, mindfulness isn't value free; it needs to be approached with a certain kind of attitude. This attitude we are trying to cultivate is a 'beginner's mind' – an openness, curiosity and receptivity to yourself as you practise mindfulness. Be patient with yourself. As I said earlier, mindfulness is not a silver bullet. I remember when I first practised mindfulness meditation; I expected a bolt from the blue – that I would immediately be filled with clarity and wisdom. Needless to say, that didn't happen. But what did happen was, for the first time in months, I felt calmer and in more wholesome mental states. I knew I had to follow this up. Over time, things changed. I changed. It's like raindrops dropping into a bowl: the amount of water in a raindrop seems insubstantial, but if they keep gathering incrementally, pretty soon there is a full bowl of still, cool water.

How to use the mindfulness exercises

When you come to a mindfulness exercise, you can read through the instructions once to give you the gist. Then you can follow the instructions, which are also broken down point by point so that you can keep referring back to them during the exercise. Or you may choose to be led through the exercises, in which case you can download the recordings from https://www.crownhouse.co.uk/mindful-teacher. You can put these on your tablet or phone, which means that they are portable and you can use them whenever you need to. After a while you may choose to self-lead, which is fine. You can set a timer on your phone with bells (see the Resources section at back of the book) or position a small clock so you can see the time.

School communities and case studies

Towards the end of the book, there are ideas and suggestions of how you can start bringing mindfulness into the classroom, once you have established your own practice through engaging with the exercises consistently.

There is also discussion about how to bring mindfulness into a work environment and become a mindfulness champion, and there are some case studies to give different examples of how this can work.

This is a handbook

Often, at the end of a mindfulness course, many participants report that now they are ready to learn mindfulness. All the anxiety about whether this works, whether this will help them, what people will think of them, has dropped away and their minds feel clear, open and receptive. The end is just the beginning – or if that's a bit too philosophical, mindfulness, like educating, is life-long learning.

This is a handbook for you to use whenever, wherever you need it. It's a chance to revisit the ideas, re-engage with practices and, most importantly, go back to sections that have seemed powerful or pertinent to you. There is space for you to make your own notes, to reflect on your own learning. As we know from our education work, ownership of learning is key to it becoming real. It is so easy to be enthusiastic at the time, but then forget until the need becomes pressing again. This book is here for you and can be a constant companion, like one you might have discovered on behaviour management or assessment. No matter how many times you forget or wander off, you can come back to this book for guidance. So make it your own – scribble on it, bend pages back, mark pages with Post-it notes, let it become tattered and dog-eared from carrying it around in your bag. It's something to anchor you and hold you steady. Because for mindfulness to be effective, for it to change your life, it's got to be done consistently.

Or as Ruby Wax eloquently puts it, 'And the bitch of it is, you have to do it every day'.[21]

---

21   R. Wax, What's so funny about mental illness?, *TED Talks* (2012). Available at: https://www.ted. com/talks/ruby_wax_what_s_so_funny_about_mental_illness?language=en.

Chapter 1

Creating the Weather in the Classroom

Finding Calm

Have you ever considered that how you are – your mood and associated behaviours and responses – is a huge influencing factor on the atmosphere of the classroom? Often, you're not fully conscious of your moods, and yet they have an effect on others. By becoming mindful of your *internal weather*, you can make a difference between being a calm breeze or whipping up a storm in the classroom.

This chapter will give you lots of tools to become aware and work with what you find. You'll learn how mindfulness can help you set a course for the day, rather than be buffeted about by worldly winds.

Centring the weather vane

Studies show that your thoughts aren't separate from your emotions.[1] Emotions, *how you are feeling*, tend to colour your thoughts, views, judgement of people, things and events. But sometimes it's hard to know how you're feeling, especially in a busy environment like a school. It can feel like you are being bombarded from the moment you walk in, until the moment you walk out, with very little space for introspection. But emotions, *your mood*, can affect your lessons, your interactions, your relationships and how well your day goes. So it pays to have some awareness of them. We're not talking in-depth counselling here; but becoming aware of your mood, *your internal weather*, can really help in making choices that mean your day going more smoothly.

---

1   Z. Segal, J. Teasdale and M. Williams, *Mindfulness-Based Cognitive Therapy for Depression*, 2nd edition (New York: Guilford Press, 2013).

What I found was when I was practising mindfulness was there was just a sense of calm. Almost all the thoughts that are going on in your head all the time, they just settled a bit and I found it easier to get through the working day really. I had the feeling of being in control and not having things happen to you. It was a bit of a mental space.

(Mike, primary school teacher)

Tuning in

- Spend a few minutes just tuning in to how you're doing. This can be done sitting in your car before leaving or arriving for work.

- Close your eyes, or have a soft gaze, and ask yourself, 'What's my internal weather right now?'

- An image might come to you, like a rain cloud or a hazy sky. Or you might have some sense of mood – sunny, stormy, bright or dull. Be patient, you might not get an immediate response.

- Whatever you find, it's important not to judge this state. Acknowledging it gives you information and from there you can decide what would be helpful today. In this way, you can start to make choices about your day.

- Gently open your eyes if they've been closed, or refocus, to the broader environment around you.

- Whatever you've discovered, try not to fix this mood, to think that's how it always is or always will be. Your moods are like weather systems; they can blow through and change.

What did you notice?

- What was the initial forecast or mood?

- What happened as you gently acknowledged it – did it stay the same or change? Again, it doesn't matter which, just notice.

Why this matters

Giving yourself a bit of space at the start of, or during, the school day can make all the difference to how positive and purposeful you feel. Often, when you focus on your mood, or how you're feeling, if you perceive it to be negative then there's immediately a sense of judgement. You think you should or shouldn't be feeling like this, you may want to push it away. Or you may focus on what you need to do to 'fix' it, to 'turn that frown upside down'. But think of a snow globe: when you shake a snow globe, there's a blizzard with snow flying everywhere. You can't see anything clearly. That's how your mind can feel sometimes; all over the place. You think it shouldn't be like this and that you need to do something to change it. However, if you just leave the snow globe, the snow will gradually fall to the bottom and settle. It's the same with your mind: if you acknowledge what's going on and give yourself a bit of internal space, anything you're feeling will just naturally calm and settle.

Coming to your senses

- Take a piece of dried fruit, a small piece of chopped fruit or some other healthy snack.

- Cultivate a strong silence; a weak silence is when it's imposed – you're told to be quiet. A strong silence is when you're naturally curious about your experience.

- Put the snack in the palm of your hand. Feel the weight of it. How does it feel? Light, heavy, different from what you expected?

- Then pick it up with the thumb and forefinger in a pincer movement, and really start to explore it with the sense of sight. Look at it as if you've never seen it before (because you haven't actually seen this exact piece of fruit before!).

- What do you notice? Depending on what you have, it may be dull or shiny, dry or moist, it might have little grooves or different tints. Spend a moment really exploring it with your sense of sight.

- Then bring it up to your nostril and take a sniff. What can you smell? It may have a strong or subtle fragrance or aroma. It might be that the smell arouses a memory for you, perhaps Christmas cake if it's a raisin. Don't try and conjure anything up, just notice what's there.

- Then rest it on your lip and notice what happens. Perhaps you sense the temperature, either coolness or warmth, or it feels dry or wet against your lips. Maybe having the food close to your lips means you can feel some tingling in the lips, as the nerves are activated with the suggestion of eating. Or perhaps you notice some saliva being produced in the mouth.

- Pop it in your mouth and then take one, big, intentional bite. What happens? Maybe an explosion of juice or flavour. Then slowly, as slowly as you can, start to chew and eat the snack, noticing the process that is making this happen:

  - the teeth biting down.

▦ the flavour being released.

▦ the sense of something quite solid becoming more liquid.

▦ the tongue moving around the mouth to facilitate the process.

Notice the impulse to swallow and when you feel ready, swallowing.

What happens then?

▦ The tongue cleaning between the teeth?

▦ The sense of absence of the snack in the mouth or a sense of aftertaste in the mouth?

▦ The feeling of wanting more?

There's no right way to do this exercise, it's just what you notice. In the table that follows you can jot down what you experienced.

What did you notice?

Sight	Touch	Smell	Taste	Anything else?

You may have noticed one sensation – such as taste, touch or smell – more intensely than the others. You may have noticed that your mind wandered off for some of the exercise but that you were able to bring it back, at least for some of the time. Perhaps you were eating differently, savouring the flavour in a way that you don't normally. Usually we are halfway through a bag of dried fruit or chocolate before we've tasted it, and this is because much of our lives are lived on autopilot.

Why this matters:
autopilot and mindfulness

Autopilot is an extremely useful function. It means that every time you get in your car, you remember how to drive it without having to consciously check the mirrors, signal, then manoeuvre, as when you are learning. Or when you step into the road and there's a car coming towards you, you know to step back. One definition of autopilot is acting or functioning without conscious thought, as a result of routine or habit. Another is a machine that keeps an aircraft on a set course without the intervention of a pilot.[2] These definitions are helpful as they really give the sense of something else driving the action, without the benefit of consciousness. Autopilot can take over so that it feels like you're going through the motions without being really there; life can start to feel mechanical. You may find yourself still rushing around, even when you're not working and really don't need to. Or you can't seem to slow down or switch off.

John Lennon said, 'Life is what happens to you while you're busy making other plans'.[3] This is autopilot in a nutshell: your life is happening right here and now, but you're not really showing up for it, you're not present to it. So how can mindfulness help?

Take your mind back to the 'Coming to your senses' exercise. For some of that time, you were able to pay attention to the eating. You did this by focusing on the senses: the smell, taste, touch of the snack. Your mind may have wandered, but you were able to bring it back, even momentarily. The snack might have been tastier or blander than you first thought, its texture might have been smoother or more defined, or it might have been wet or dry. That's how it was, that's how you experienced it. And while you did it, even though your mind wandered, you may have found yourself more in the present, rather than thinking about the future or the past. Life is a series of present moments. So, a definition of mindfulness is paying attention, with the senses, in the present moment, to things as they are.

However, mindfulness is not something that happens in a vacuum and is value free. The quality of mindfulness, of how you pay attention, really matters. Because, as Professor Mark Williams discusses, an assassin is very mindful.[4] They have razor-sharp focus and split-second timing. But that's not quite the quality you are looking for here. You may think of mindfulness as something like a surveillance camera – a naked, cold observation that records everything that you are doing. But it's not like that at all.

---

2   See https://www.oed.com/view/Entry/249989.
3   John Lennon, Beautiful boy (darling boy) (Geffen Records, 1980).
4   D. Penman and M. Williams, *Finding Peace in a Frantic World* (London: Piatkus, 2011).

Mindfulness has a warm, inclusive, curious and even playful quality. It's about culti-vating an attitude of kindness towards yourself, rather than harsh self-criticism. Think of how a young child explores the world: they often have a natural sense of wonder, they ask curious questions. The past or the future mean nothing to them. They are fully absorbed in the present.

The other thing to note is there's nothing particularly spiritual about a piece of dried fruit or a snack; they're everyday objects. But by paying attention to these objects and what you're doing, when you're doing it, the quality of our awareness changes. If the quality of awareness changes, the quality of your life can change. If your life is hap-pening while you're busy doing other things, and if life is a series of present moments, wouldn't it be good to show up for some of them?

> It was the fact that I could just be and do something which perhaps I didn't think I could do previously. Immediately it made me feel calmer and notice what was going on. Whereas I realised before I'd been living on autopilot, that was when big things started to happen for me.
>
> (Belle, early years teacher)

This not only matters for you but also for others. You're not the only one who will have internal weather: fellow colleagues, pupils and parents will all have their own weather systems going on too. Unless you're aware, there may be an electrical charge between you and them, leading to unnecessary confrontation, conflict or misunder-standing. Research shows us that the impact of our social environment is ongoing; we are constantly being shaped by, and shaping, others. By having some awareness of what your internal weather is and giving it some space to settle, it will have an effect on staff and students around you. It will send a signal to their nervous systems that they can begin to calm down and settle too.[5] A systematic review of 13 studies on mind-fulness-based interventions showed that emotional regulation – *managing the internal weather*, bringing greater awareness to thoughts, emotions and mood and how they play out physically in the body or action – is the aspect of mindfulness practice that staff find most helpful.[6]

Some teachers have found that, with time and practice, awareness of your mind and body becomes like a pedagogy.

---

5   L. Flook, S. B. Goldberg, L. Pinger, K. Bonus and R. J. Davidson, Mindfulness for teachers: a pilot study to assess effects on stress, burnout, and teaching efficacy, *Mind, Brain, and Education* 7 (2013): 182–195.

6   Y. Hwang, B. Bartlett, M. Greben and K. Hand, A systematic review of mindfulness interventions for in-service teachers: a tool to enhance teacher wellbeing and performance, *Teaching and Teacher Education* 64 (2017): 26–42.

It's like a teaching method, slowing down the pace, the voice, everything that you're doing. Being aware of the effect that you have on the children and noticing the effect that it has when you don't do this.

(Jo, primary school teacher)

Stepping out of autopilot

These are mindfulness exercises to try in the week – to become aware of, and work with, your internal weather and bring calm.

Emotional barometer

Our emotions often show up in our body.

▦ Tune in. Once you have some sense of your internal weather, scan your upper body (crown of the head to bottom of pelvis).

▦ Notice if there's any place that's coming to your attention: a tightness somewhere or tension.

▦ Take your awareness to that place and notice the sensations there.

▦ Then take three intentional breaths (in and out) directed at this area.

▦ What happens now?

Finger breathing – a tool to calm

This is a simple exercise to focus and calm you.

- With one finger, trace up one side and down the other of the fingers on the opposite hand.

- When you've finished, loop back round to start again, or swap hands.

- Notice the touch between the contact of the fingers.

- If you like you can synchronise the breathing, breathing in as you trace up and out as you trace down. But if this feels too artificial, feel free to let the breath come and go.

- Once you've mastered this, you can do it anywhere, like under the desk during a challenging class or meeting. Nobody needs to know you are doing it.

Use the following space to journal about which exercises you did in the chapter and what you noticed. You can include days when you didn't manage to do any and what the impact of that was.

What did you do?	What did you notice?	How did you feel before/after?

In this chapter, you've learnt about:

- How to create the weather in the classroom, but you can become more aware of yourself and learn to manage this.

- What mindfulness is and its qualities.

- The function of being on autopilot, and how it's great for some things but not if it takes over.

- How mindfulness can bring you back to your senses and our present-moment experience.

Chapter 2
Breaking Up Is Never Easy

The Art of Making Transitions
in the School Day

To build on the last chapter and increase your awareness during the school day, let's take a look at transitions. Examples of transitions are: leaving the car to enter the school, going from lesson to lesson, before or after yard duty, going from communicating with a group such as a class or staff meeting to more focused communication with one other person like a pupil or parent. Making transitions in the school day can be difficult – with so many events and decisions happening quickly, your mind is constantly being shaped by what's gone before or anticipating what's to come. So how can you stay focused and fresh?

> You know that feeling when you know you feel really stressed and then it's really hard to get out of that. Sometimes there'll be a phone call or message to ring a parent and you think, well I've got to deal with that. Some kid comes in or someone's fallen over or you can't find the resource that you want and suddenly you're in a real whirlwind.
>
> (Michael, primary school teacher)

It's no wonder you may feel compressed, blank out or feel overwhelmed. After weeks of days of this at school, it's easy to end up feeling exhausted, dissatisfied, regretful or mentally drained. So let's have a look at how mindfulness can help you manage the school day and transitions better.

Transitions can feel painful – you may have to peel yourself away from an event you have enjoyed, like teaching your favourite year group, and face something less appetising, such as yard duty. On the other hand, it can feel like a relief to get away from an experience such as a lesson that has been unpleasant and on to something that will hopefully feel a bit better. Or you may already feel full up from what's happened so far in the day, so there is a daze or confusion in your mind about what's coming next.

Whichever it is, it's during these transitions that autopilot tends to kick in most strongly. With no space to think or act differently, habit tends to take over. As we discussed in the first chapter, autopilot is a useful strategy for some things, but if it becomes your modus operandi, then life can feel mechanical and you'll be less effective. Also, when you're in autopilot, you're more likely to react, because your actions are automatic. Reacting is that knee-jerk response – without thinking, you do what you've always done and hope for the best.

Mindfulness allows a more thoughtful and creative option to emerge. To access this you need to give yourself some space, to step out of autopilot. That's why engaging with transitions mindfully can become a moment of clarity, sustenance or resetting yourself. Transitions are a natural part of life – each moment is constantly unfolding from the next, so there's an opportunity. But you need your wits about you.

The first way that mindfulness can help is acknowledging the transition: things are changing, you are moving from one activity to the next. This doesn't need to take long, just a conscious registering that this is what's happening (whether you like it or not).

Next, you need to create some space for yourself, no matter what time constraint you have. You can spend a moment feeling your feet on the floor, focusing exclusively on the breath, checking in with yourself and noticing how you're doing. You can ask yourself, 'What's my internal weather right now? Sunny, rainy, dull or bright?' That gives you information about what you need to do and how you need to do it, next.

Susan is an experienced teacher in a busy secondary school:

> There's this staff toilet, where you can lock it from the inside and I know that's a space where I cannot be interrupted for two minutes. So I take my time, wash my hands, dry them, feeling my feet on the floor and just build in a little routine of mindfully walking back up the corridor to my classroom. It's enough to reset, to deal with that overwhelming feeling of *I can't cope with this,* I can't cope with the next lesson.' Realising that's overthinking and just giving myself that space.

Other ways to create a mindful transition are: if clearing up at the end of the lesson and on your own, you could choose to stretch or take a few breaths, rather than rushing blindly into the next activity. When eating lunch you can just focus on tasting or enjoy the company of colleagues as you do so, rather than wolfing it down in front of the computer. At the start of the day when you're arranging the class, you can spend a few moments tuning in to set yourself up for the day. All these are very simple practices that won't take very long, but they do make a difference. You can do these in a few minutes, or seconds if needed!

You need to stop and give yourself a moment. It sounds simple but a lot of people don't do it.

(Claire, safeguarding and well-being manager, FE college)

Of course, the main resistance towards doing this will be the thought that there's no time. Teachers may feel self-conscious about taking a few moments to themselves because of the pressures in the school day. But the question is, what do we lose if we don't allow ourselves this short amount of time? Chances are that you will feel rushed along by the tide of the school day with little choice or agency, which brings about its own frustrations or resentments. If you push yourself through on autopilot, mistakes can be made, you forget things, you can react to a child or colleague in such a way that then takes time to resolve. Or you just feel overwhelmed and therefore cannot think clearly. A few minutes spent mindfully during the day can save time in all sorts of ways later on.

Anthony teaches in a secondary school:

I think – am I present? Am I really here? There are all these things going on but I still need to get them done. In a nuts and bolts activity, I'll think, let's be present, let's go for a mindful walk around the classroom. Let's come back to it. I've got a 100 things to mark and my mind's all over the place. Let's do just 5, go for a mindful walk, come back and do 5. These little techniques are great, they work.

Why this matters:
from doing to being mode

A few years ago Ladybird, a much-loved children's book brand, published various parodies, one of which was *The Ladybird Book of Mindfulness*. The character on the front cover is a long-haired hippy, wafting around in a field. Inside, one of the scenarios reads:

Alison has been staring at this beautiful tree for five hours. She was meant to be in the office, tomorrow she will be fired. In this way mindfulness will have resolved her work related stress![1]

This captures the stereotype about mindfulness, that you have to stop doing everything and do nothing. However, practising mindfulness isn't about doing nothing. But it is

---

1   J. Hazeley and J. Morris, *The Ladybird Book of Mindfulness* (London: Michael Joseph, 2015), p. 22.

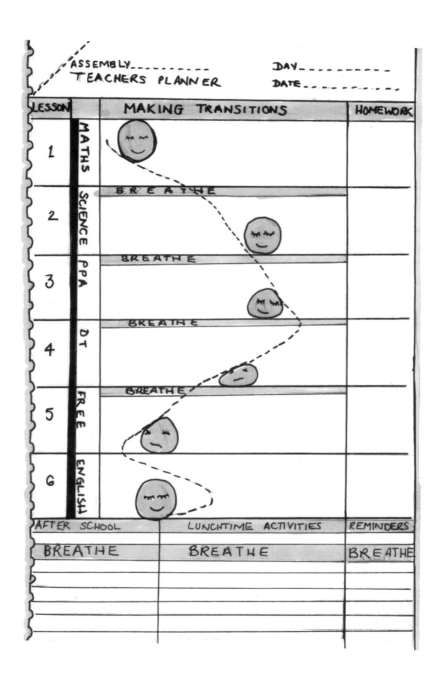

about stepping away from a *driven* doing mode. The driven doing mode is fuelled by autopilot – you feel driven and compulsively do things or think you should be doing them. You can't seem to stop yourself and find it hard to switch off. The worst thing about it is that you might know rationally that these things don't *have* to be done right now. But you are in the grip of frenetic activity. It's no wonder so many people fantasise about retiring, a time when you can finally have some peace and quiet.

However, there is an alternative to the driven doing mode, which is a mindful being mode. But that doesn't mean giving everything up and doing nothing, like the woman in the scenario. The being mode means that you give yourself some time to be, even while you are doing. You notice when you are feeling driven and stop, do a short mindfulness practice to recentre and ground yourself, and then carry on. You may have to do this several times a day, but it means you will carry on with your day feeling more contented and purposeful rather than ineffective and ragged. Like any new habit, it takes practice, but the more you practise, the more it will come naturally.

This is why it's really important to see transitions as an opportunity to step out of driven doing mode and into mindful being mode. A perfect way to punctuate your day with a mindful pause is 'The mindful minute' exercise.

The mindful minute

Everyone has a minute. Set a timer on your phone or use the minute hand on your watch. In a minute, see how many whole breaths (in and out) that you take. Breathe naturally, don't change your breath and just count how many you do in that minute. It doesn't matter how many. Just note them down. Now you know how many breaths you take in a minute – if it was 12, for example, you just take that number of breaths consciously when making a transition. Or do them anytime you feel stressed or overwhelmed.

Of course, practising mindfulness during transitions during the school day isn't the only place you can do it; you can do it in other areas of your life, too. So in the run-up to the day you can allow yourself to come into the world of the senses: when you have a shower or drink a cup of coffee, really notice the sensations, the taste, the temperature, and enjoy them. You can connect with your children, partner or pet when they wake up or be present when you're making their packed lunch/feeding them. On the drive to work, you can notice indications of the changing seasons in the trees or wholeheartedly sing along to your favourite tune! All these help you feel calmer, more grounded and ready to face the day. You may do these things already, but give yourself permission to really value them as an important part of your day.

At the end of the school day, if you feel exhausted and spent, you are more liable to be in autopilot and to react. It's unfortunate that many people who give to others professionally during the day don't feel they have the time or energy to give to their loved ones. However, you can use these transitions to change modes. I used to give myself a few moments, sitting in the car, acknowledging that I was making a transition into home life now. You can spend a few minutes breathing and checking in with yourself before you enter your home. At home, do something deliberate to signal to yourself that you're changing modes, such as having a cup of tea or spending a bit of time in the garden. If you live with other people, be curious about them, ask them what their day has been like, focusing on them. In turn, take the opportunity to say how your day has been. Although simple, all these steps can help make the transition from *driven doing mode* to *mindful being mode* and have an energising effect.

Mindfulness is not a magic wand to life's troubles – but just by becoming aware and giving space to the unfolding nature of your experience, life can feel more purposeful, satisfying and fun!

Along with the mindful minute, here are some exercises to help you manage the transitions before, after or during the school day.

Stepping out of autopilot:
the routine activity

Choose one activity that you would normally do every day – for example, brushing your teeth, having a shower, drinking a cup of tea, eating a meal or snack. Pay a bit more attention to it as you do it, come into the senses – what do you notice?

For example, if it's brushing your teeth, notice the sensation of the brush against the teeth, the taste of the toothpaste, the water splashing. If it's an electric toothbrush, notice the sound. Choose one activity and follow it through for a week, rather than chopping and changing it. Don't worry if one day you forget to do it, just come back to it the next day.

Eat one meal or snack mindfully in the week.

Take your time and savour each mouthful.

What did you notice?

Become conscious of transitions in the school day over a week, and bring awareness to them as best you can, using the practices suggested or others that work for you. Note down three times in the day that you managed/didn't manage to do this. What was the benefit/the cost?

Day: three times when you did/didn't manage a mindful transition	What did you do?	What was the benefit/cost?
Day 1		
Day 2		
Day 3		
Day 4		
Day 5		

Why this matters

The unrelenting nature of a school means that autopilot can easily take over and you end up rushing to the next activity, contributing to you feeling exhausted at some point in the school day. It's in the transitions, from moment to moment, that there's an opportunity to become more grounded, focused and energised. You can notice the transition and choose to make it a moment of calm and resetting. These pauses have power; they remind you that each moment is a new opportunity to start again. In this way you can start to step out of the driven doing mode into mindful being mode. This is a new habit and will take time to establish but will be well worth it. The main argument for choosing mindfulness and awareness during transitions is that awareness changes everything. Once you realise that you can cultivate this faculty then your whole experience can change. The fabric of life becomes different – lighter, more vibrant, finer.

In this chapter, you've learnt:

- How to make the school day less of a grind, by using transitions as an opportunity to step out of driven doing mode and into mindful being mode.

- If you don't take these opportunities, autopilot will take over, and you may become exhausted and reactive, causing yourself more difficulty.

- The mindful minute is simple to do but can make all the difference, as can the other mindful practices in this chapter.

Chapter 3
Behaviour Management

Responding, not Reacting

Behaviour management is a key classroom skill: you're the coach, the classroom is the training pitch and the students are the players. Some will participate willingly, some will foul their opponents and some will oscillate between the two. There are already lots of theories and books covering a variety of classroom behaviour management strategies, so this chapter specifically focuses on how mindfulness can aid successful behaviour management. Ultimately, this comes down to one thing: responding, not reacting.

The classroom can be an ecosystem, where an incident or change can affect the whole balance. Reacting is what you do when you are on autopilot, as discussed in Chapter 1. When I first started teaching in a further education college, I was given a group, some of whose behaviour was, at times, pretty awful. It was a shock to the system, trying to get a grip on bouts of unruly and rude behaviour. As many of us do when we are in shock, I went into fight, flight and freeze mode. My shoulders would tense, my throat tighten and I would become rigid both in body and attitude. I would arrive home feeling exhausted. I was reacting. I knew that this wasn't sustainable and that I wasn't going to last long in teaching if I carried on in this way. I needed to be able to be more flexible, both physically and mentally.

Responding, rather than reacting, involves awareness – awareness on different levels. You can approach these levels of awareness in terms of self, other, environment and the bigger picture. Let's look at them one by one.

Awareness of self

The practices suggested in the book so far all build an awareness of self: of how you are, physically, mentally and emotionally. For example, when I was teaching the college class I mentioned above, I also had a 1-year-old baby at home and was sleep deprived. This led to its own tension, a sense of starting the day tired and feeling like I had to push on through. That meant I was bringing more tension to an already stressful situation. As a result, checking in with my body during the day became crucial – for example, every time I noticed my shoulders were tense or my jaw was clenched, I simply softened them, and this released energy. The emotional barometer is a good exercise to help with this. Going back to Chapter 2, I started doing the mindful minute before the start of a class, to prepare and limber up. These are practices that can be done quickly, with eyes open, and nobody need know that you are doing them. Working in a secondary school or college can feel unrelenting, as one class leaves and another one arrives. But, by using the simple strategies suggested in Chapter 2, feeling your feet on the floor and taking a few conscious breaths as the class file in and take their seats can make all the difference.

When you are on autopilot, there is a tendency to overreact; something quite mild, such as a pupil's abrupt reply, sullen attitude or rolling of the eyes, can be magnified and potentially escalate into a low-level conflict situation. This draws the attention of the rest of the class, who will welcome distraction or a bit of drama.

> Years ago I used to do this assertive discipline approach, telling the student: 'You've chosen to stay in at break time because you've chosen not to listen.' But I was taking a stand-off position and this created distance between me and the class.
>
> (Mike, primary school teacher)

Responding means being grounded and having a broader perspective that takes in all factors, including yourself. So, when something disruptive happens:

- Notice your body – are you tensing?

- Notice your breath – are you holding the breath? (This is something we are likely to do when we are trying to be in control.)

- Can you feel your feet on the floor before speaking?

You might be saying now, 'I don't have time for that, the class will be in chaos!' But it only takes a few seconds, whereas an escalation or conflict between you and a student will take much longer to sort out. A systematic review on mindfulness for teachers based on 16 reviews concluded that mindfulness helps teachers/school staff change their relationship with their experience, including an increased ability to examine perceptions before reacting. This opened up new possibilities of choice.[1]

> I know I was always quick to react. If there was a problem in the class, I wanted to get it sorted so the children could go back to their work. But now I think it's more important to wait and see the whole thing. Pausing is something that has been effective. A lot of the research shows that what a lot of children in high-stress situations need is calmness. I thought I was calm before, but I wasn't.

> (Jan, primary school teacher)

Awareness of other

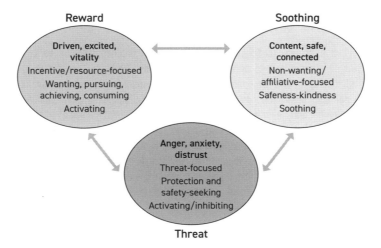

Three systems of emotional regulation (adapted from Gilbert, *The Compassionate Mind*, p. 24)

In my experience, there is always some reason for bad behaviour. Going back to the group I mentioned at the start of the chapter, at the beginning of my teaching career I felt shocked by this kind of behaviour. It was rude, disrespectful and unacceptable in a learning environment. I felt on the back foot and I made the mistake of taking it

---

1   Hwang et al., A systematic review of mindfulness interventions for in-service teachers.

personally, thinking it was something to do with me and my teaching. After a while, I realised it was about them; they were terrified. A lot of the students had had an unsatisfactory experience at school. They came into college with that baggage; they were fearful of failure or being shown up in front of their peers. Once I worked that out, while not accepting the behaviour, I was not reacting to it in the same way. With some empathy and understanding to their point of view, I could respond using a number of different strategies.

Professor Paul Gilbert, a practising clinical psychologist and professor at the University of Derby, identified in his book *The Compassionate Mind* that humans have three main systems of emotional regulation: threat, reward and soothing.[2] It's important to state that we need all three; they're simply what we do when we are triggered by thoughts, feelings, other people or situations. Let's take a closer look at them.

Threat: This system is all about keeping safe. Whether the threat is real or perceived, the sympathetic nervous system is triggered to either fight, flight or freeze – physically and mentally. You will do what you have always done or learnt to do in order to keep yourself safe. Your senses narrow to focus on the threat, and your body and brain are flooded with adrenaline and cortisol in order to ensure your survival.

Reward: This is the ability to focus on and pursue projects/tasks where you will be rewarded. You get a buzz out of achieving your goals. This is a very useful mindset for projects or tasks where you need to hunker down and focus. However, it can become addictive; you pursue task after task in a driven way, seeking external confirmation of your inner self-worth. Game-creators exploit this drive when they create different gaming content – it's about the gamers being driven to achieve the next level and not being willing to give up until they do. The hormone associated with this circle is dopamine – the hit or the buzz you feel when you achieve. The difficulty is when you don't achieve, when your efforts are thwarted; for example, maybe you had an idea of how the lesson was going to go and it hasn't. You can feel annoyed, frustrated, blame others or yourself and easily switch into the threat zone.

Soothing: This is your ability to self-soothe, and it goes right back to being a baby and those feelings of safety, warmth and connection you had when you bonded with a caregiver. It connects into the parasympathetic nervous system, which creates the ability to calm down and centre yourself. This is what self-regulation means from a nervous-system point of view, and teachers report that there are greater numbers of students in the class who are unable to self-regulate. The mindfulness practices you have learnt so far improve your ability to self-soothe and self-regulate. The hormone

---

2   P. Gilbert, *The Compassionate Mind* (London: Constable, 2010), p. 24.

associated with this circle is oxytocin – that feeling of connection and that things will be OK.

As previously stated, it's not that any of the states illustrated by these circles are wrong, they are what happen at any given time depending on emotional triggers. Nor is it that you should try to live permanently in one circle. It's more about becoming aware of which one you are in, and deciding if that's what will help you right now – and if not, being able to move into a different circle. So, for example, when a behaviour incident happens, you may immediately be in the threat zone. If there is a genuine danger of harm to you or the students, then that's appropriate. But if not, then you may be escalating the situation. You may feel that your authority is being questioned, that you're not being respected – and this digs you further into the threat zone. The student in question may have had a blazing row with their parents before school or the night before, or there may be friendship issues or something that's upset them on social media. They are in the threat zone, too. If you both lock horns then there will be a struggle. Somebody has to stand down and de-escalate. And, unfortunately, being the adult in the room, that has to be you!

It's time to be flexible – because if the student is in the threat zone, then perhaps they can't self-regulate and they need someone to do that for them. You need to change the weather in the classroom, as explored in Chapter 1. Feel your feet on the floor, take a breath, change the tone of your voice. All this will help the student come back into relationship with you and others. Check out your understanding or assumption about what is happening, ask a question and be genuinely curious about their answer. I remember being so wound up by a class that when I finally got them to task, a student asked a question and I reacted, misperceiving her to be disruptive. Looking back, she was asking a genuine, clarifying question – but because of what had gone before, I couldn't see that clearly. She was trying to get on with her work, behaviour that is usually rewarded but I didn't recognise that. So you need to calm yourself in the moment and embody that calm for others.

> Sometimes, when children are off task and misbehaving, that's like a threat to me because it threatens my sense of authority. You can sort of take it personally, but I have since learnt to step away from that a little bit and think, 'They're just children. They're not misbehaving because my lesson planning's bad or my lesson's boring.'
>
> (Mike, primary school teacher)

This is not to say that there are not consequences to bad behaviour or to take away any mandates, but just recognising that sometimes conflict and unpleasantness can be stoked unnecessarily. Are you prone to taking things too personally? As Mike says, 'They're just children'.

This can apply to your colleagues too. Maybe they are having a bad day or have been triggered by something. They may snap at you or be abrupt. Notice if you are taking it personally. It might be personal, but very often it's not. If you can stay grounded and calm and move towards them, they will appreciate it. Often, when someone is triggered by stress, a kind word or action can make all the difference. This can move someone into the soothing circle of the emotional regulation system.

Awareness of environment

At the beginning of the chapter, I spoke about the teacher being the coach and the students being the players. But there is also the learning environment: the pitch. It's easy to overlook this, but environment can play a key part in both containing what's happening with behaviour and also having a broader perspective. Most trainee teachers/lecturers will learn about Maslow's hierarchy of needs (1968).[3] Maslow teaches that until basic needs are met – food, water, shelter and safety – then learning or self-development can't really take place. So take a moment to take the temperature of the class – is it too hot or cold? Are the students too crowded together? Is there a way in which you could space them out more, or set up the room for more cooperative learning? Are the walls looking drab? Could they be brightened up with students' work that could instil feelings of pride and be a motivating factor? It can be difficult in a secondary school or college where you are moving from room to room, but a few minutes taking in and setting up the environment can pay off later in terms of learning and motivation. The learning environment can also act as the container. If I poured an egg cup of salt into a glass of water and took a sip, that water is going to taste very salty. But if I poured the same amount into a five-litre container of water, the taste would be much milder. It's the same with the classroom: the more you can keep your awareness on the bigger picture and whole-class environment, the less drawn in you can become to specific incidents and lose perspective.

When a behavioural incident or disruption happens, you can automatically perceive threat and narrow in on the incident. You want to solve it, to fix the problem and for it to go away. By doing this, are you losing perspective? Keeping a broad awareness of the rest of the class may show you that they are getting on with their work quite happily. Without this, there's a tendency to leap in.

> In my classroom, if there'd be a couple of kids off task, what I used to do was to go right in and say, 'What are you doing? Get back to work!' Now, however, I just remind myself to stop and I just watch. I bring curiosity: what's going on here? And sometimes they just get back to work or they'll look at me and there's been no disruption to the flow of the lesson and that's really nice. So I'm getting better at just standing back a bit.
>
> (Mike, primary school teacher)

When you react, you tend to get sucked in. When I used to do this, it was as if it was only myself and the disruptive student in the room. But what about the other 29 students?

---

3 A. Rogers, Maslow hierarchy of needs. In *Teaching Adults*, 3rd edition (Oxford: Oxford University Press, 2002), p. 96.

What value was I placing on their learning and well-being by allowing myself to be drawn in by the disruptive student?

So if you notice yourself doing this, keep your gaze broad and wide. Make eye contact with other students, check in with how they are doing, remind the disruptive student that they are in relationship with the rest of the class. Other students might make a helpful comment or defuse the situation if you give them space, and students tend to care more what their peers think than their teachers. This may help de-escalate the situation because, in my experience, once a student has the laser beam of your focus on them, it can lead them to react even worse – either because they need the attention or because they suddenly feel exposed and self-conscious. So become that bigger container – use the space and the environment of the classroom as a support against reacting.

Awareness of the bigger picture

Responding requires your life experience, your wisdom and intuition. It encompasses what you've learnt so far about how people like to be treated and what they are likely to respond positively to. Sometimes this means walking the path of humility; you do get it wrong sometimes. This may happen in the moment or later on in the day, the next day or when you have a bit of space to reflect. During the year of teaching the group I have mentioned, I did apologise to them on a couple of occasions. They were clearly 'gob-smacked' at this, that someone in a position of authority could admit error and valued them enough to seek forgiveness. The atmosphere in the group softened – and having modelled this, I noticed that they were more forgiving of their own slip-ups too.

You may fear that this approach will make you look weak, but it in fact takes courage and this will come across. In my experience, students respond to the truth and respect you for it. They also learn a powerful life lesson about repairing and maintaining relationships.

The truth is that no one can be completely objective – you all have your triggers and biases. I have misinterpreted and misperceived the actions of others countless times. So there is wisdom in giving the benefit of the doubt. It might be through reflecting, days, weeks or months later, when you can clearly see what was happening and can admit your own part.

When an incident happens, there can be a tendency to berate yourself or engage in harsh self-criticism and ruminate about what went wrong. But this will sap your energy and resources even more. Imagine how you would respond to a close colleague who recounted the same incident to you? Would you be critical and unkind? You are deserving of kindness and understanding too. Ultimately, responding means being able to come to each moment afresh, without carrying the baggage of what's gone before. So forgive yourself. Tomorrow is another day.

Mindfulness exercises to try

The three-step breathing space

This is a really quick and portable practice that you can use to ground and reset yourself. You can use it before a class or after a difficult/disruptive incident to come back and centre yourself.

It can be as long as you like – whether it be 3 minutes or 10 seconds – depending on how much time is available to you.

- Step 1: Acknowledge – check in with yourself, scan the body for any tightness and tension, tune in to your internal weather (mood), feel your feet firmly on the floor.

- Step 2: Gather – focus your attention around the breath. Keep the breath normal and natural but keep your concentration on it – on both the in breath and the out breath.

- Step 3: Expand – widen your awareness back out from the breath to take in the whole of you sitting here, your physicality, posture, what you can see and hear.

You're good to go! This is another effective practice to move from driven doing to mindful being mode.

Experiment with using the three-step breathing space during transitions, as explored in Chapter 2 and after any difficult incident/episode.

What did you notice?

_____

_____

_____

_____

_____

Why does this matter?

The three-step breathing space is a quick and easy way to reset yourself when things are busy, difficult or you need a moment of calm. Often, you accept things far too readily and think, 'This is how it is, this is how I am'. But that is your autopilot speaking. Awareness rises and changes moment by moment, and if you consciously plug into it by doing the three-step breathing space, change is easier and choice becomes available.

> I found the three-step breathing space so accessible and transformational, retreating to that sense of stillness even for a short time. That's something I do really regularly, coming back to bodily sensations. Scanning my posture – why am I sitting like that? It doesn't feel good, so coming back to the body and trying to be in the body and have awareness of how I'm holding my spine, neck, for example. At the end of the day, the body wants to be well. But a lot of what we're doing is not great for the body. So even sitting in front of the computer, you can have bodily awareness, breathing,

awareness, you have the choice of how you respond to things, rather than just having a habitual response.

(Lisa, early years teacher)

When you've had a stressful day and adrenaline and cortisol are pumping through your system, it can be difficult to 'come down' and let go. This practice can really help in terms of de-stressing and coming back into some sort of balance – physically, mentally and emotionally.

Playful body scan

▓ Lie down on the floor if that's comfortable for you. You can lie on the bed or the sofa if lying on the floor is a problem.

▓ Make sure you are lying on something soft. Have a light blanket to cover yourself with as your body temperature can drop when you're lying down. Already you might be feeling cosy and that gives a signal to the nervous system that you are safe and the adrenaline will start to drop. You may feel really tired.

▓ Make sure your neck is comfortable, perhaps propping it on a pillow or cushion and if you have vulnerability in your lower back, experiment with having a pillow or cushion under the knees.

▓ Start with a broad awareness of the body on the surface you're lying on. Be curious about the points of contact between your body and the floor/bed. Where can you feel the connection? Perhaps the back of the head, the shoulder blades, back of the pelvis, calf muscles, back of the ankles?

▓ Notice if you are tensing at all, trying to notice all these parts of the body, or holding your breath, trying to get this right! Whatever you notice is fine, let the breath be normal and natural.

- Have a sense of the earth grounding you and supporting you, however you are. When you've had a stressful, busy day, the effect can be like a static energy in your nervous system. By focusing on the body, on the earth (even if you're on a bed), it's a bit like the earthing wire in an electrical plug. It gives somewhere for that static energy to discharge.

- The earth is quite capable of holding and dispersing this energy, so really let go into this contact with the surface beneath you. Take some deep breaths and on the exhalation feel your body sinking deeper into the earth and being held and cradled. This may feel really good and you just want to stay doing this, which is fine.

- If you're happy to move on, you're going to shine the spotlight of our awareness on different parts of the body and just note anything you can feel directly. Perhaps you won't feel anything and this is fine – keep your attitude light and playful, as this is not an exam you need to pass!

- So let's start with the right knee, focusing your attention lightly on the right knee. How does it feel? Tight or loose? Let your awareness rest on the right knee and just notice what you notice.

- Let go of the right knee and switch to the left ankle, the tiny muscles and bones of the left ankle. Again, notice any direct sensations like the back of the ankle pressing into the floor. If you can't feel anything, don't worry and move on.

- Now the back of the head: does the surface you're lying on feel hard or soft against the head?

- The eyes, are they moving around focusing on different objects or do they feel heavy in their sockets?

- The middle fingers on both hands, do they feel tingly, fizzy, numb or no sensation at all? What about the little fingers?

- At points during this practice, your mind will wander off – that's what your mind does and so it's only to be expected. The main thing is to accept that it will happen, notice when it does and then bring it back to the part of the body you were focusing on. Don't give yourself a hard time.

Finish by placing both hands on your belly, if that's comfortable to you, and feeling the rise and fall of the breath in this area. This can feel very comforting and you're shifting your focus away from your head and your thinking, to an area that's visceral. Let your awareness rest here, on the in and out breaths for a few breaths.

You may have been lying for a while, in which case you need to be gentle in how you change position so that you won't jar yourself or lose the body awareness you have built up.

Start by introducing a little bit of movement, such as opening and closing the hands. You may want to rock gently from side to side, just to get the body used to moving. When you feel ready, roll on one side and take a moment there, noticing the different shape of the body in this position, the different perspective you can see there. Then using the hands to push yourself up, come to sitting and gently move into standing, walking. Let it be a flow of movement.

All the parts of the body I've noted are just suggestions; you may notice other ones that are calling for your attention. If that's the case, use the same process; let your awareness rest on them and notice what you notice and then move on.

Experiment with doing this at different times of the day/week – early evening, in the morning before everyone gets up, at the weekend.

Try to make some time for yourself; you do so much for other people and you deserve to do something for yourself.

What did you notice?

Why does this matter?

Teaching is a stressful job, and after a busy day, adrenaline and cortisol are going to be flooding your body, making you feel 'tired but wired'. The playful body scan is an effective way of changing gear, from doing to being. It can be grounding but also allow that 'tired but wired' energy to be released and flow into the earth. By calming and grounding in this way you can make a transition from school and then decide, 'What would I like to do with my evening/my weekend?'

Space to journal

_____

_____

_____

_____

In this chapter, we've discussed:

- How mindfulness can enhance behaviour management strategies by helping you to respond, rather than react.

- The concepts of reacting and responding and the difference the two can make to behaviour management and relationships in the classroom.

- The framework of self, other, environment and bigger picture is useful in terms of depersonalising an interaction and looking at the conditions that can govern actions, speech and behaviour.

- How Paul Gilbert's model of the three systems of emotional regulation is helpful in terms of interpreting behaviour and acting accordingly.

- How the suggested mindfulness exercises are short ones to help you find calm in the moment, and then a longer one to help you let go and release any tension when you have the opportunity.

Chapter 4
Mindfulness for Stressful Times

For an Inspection

The dreaded phone call announcing an imminent inspection can send all school staff into a blind panic. In the anticipation of or run-up to an inspection, there can be a sustained sense of hyper-alertness and stress. Senior leaders can go into overdrive, being target and task focused and pressurising staff. Staff can worry, feel fearful and unsupported, and are more likely to go into fight, flight or freeze mode. The stakes are high, as what category the school/college is put in may have serious consequences. So how can practising mindfulness help the situation, so that everyone can cooperate and be at their best?

> Mindfulness has got me to stop and take stock. Think about where I am in that minute. What do I need to do? Prioritise what I need to do first, then I am bring pro-active.
>
> (Claire, safeguarding and well-being manager, FE college)

Kipling wrote, 'If you can keep your head when all about you are losing theirs and blaming it on you'.[1] This sentiment definitely rings true both in the run-up and during an inspection. I remember during notice of inspection in the college where I worked, receiving an email from a senior manager expressing her disgust at the state of some of the classrooms. Prior to the announcement of the inspection, she'd shown no interest in the state of the classrooms or provided any budget to change them. My colleagues and I felt angry and demoralised at receiving the email. Here we were, going above and beyond for the students and feeling anxious and fearful of the impending inspection; what we needed was encouragement.

More than anything else, an inspection, or the anticipation of one, can put a school/ college community into the threat circle (see Chapter 3). And yet to get through it, everyone needs to feel that they're working together, thriving so that they can show the school or college at its best. Obviously, this depends on the organisational culture –

---

1   R. Kipling, *A Choice of Kipling's Verse* (London: Faber, 1976).

if that cooperative and collaborative atmosphere is missing, it's not going to be sufficiently drummed up in the notice period. But whatever is going on out there, however much others are losing their heads, here's what you can do to empower yourself and keep yours.

Before the inspection

The main point to emphasise is that your health and mental well-being is your top priority. You may have a perfectionist streak, but if you get work-related stress or illness, then it will be difficult for you and everyone around you. It's also your responsibility; you cannot look to anyone else to do it for you. So it's your duty to look after yourself during this time. This starts with all the sensible things that you know will keep you well. It's worth emphasising these as they can be easily forgotten as soon as a stressful situation occurs. Are you sleeping enough? Eating healthily and making sure your blood sugar doesn't drop too low? Getting out in the fresh air and exercising? All these will have a huge effect on your mood and energy levels and stabilise you physically, emotionally and mentally. If you don't attend to these, then it's more than likely the following will happen.

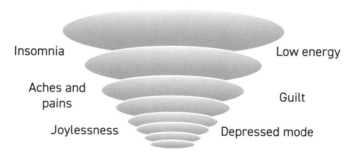

Insomnia   Low energy

Aches and pains   Guilt

Joylessness   Depressed mode

Exhaustion

The exhaustion funnel (developed by Mark Williams and Denny Penman)[2]

---

2   See http://www.mindfulnext.org/burnout-the-exhaustion-funnel.

You may recognise this diagram in your own life. When you are living a healthy, balanced life, you are in the top part of the funnel: your life consists of rest and enjoyable things as well as work. The difficulty is that when a stressful situation arises, such as an inspection, the temptation can be to cut out the enjoyable things such as hobbies and exercise, or even to cut out rest or eating properly, and just focus on work. This may be sustainable in the short term, like in the week of the inspection or if you're finishing a project or an assignment. But it's not a long-term strategy; if you narrow your life down to the demands of work then you start to lose perspective and joy. You can feel drained and exhausted and, as the model depicts, you may feel like you are starting to go down the plug hole. You could find yourself at the bottom of the funnel, and anyone who's been there knows this is a pretty grim place to be. It's far harder to try and get your health and well-being back from such a low place than to try and maintain it from a broader place, even if it isn't perfect. So you owe it to yourself to keep a broad balance of activities in your life and stay at the top of the funnel – because if you're at the bottom, you can't be there for your family, children, colleagues and young people in your care.

> I know that so much crisis management goes on at school with behaviour of children, the parents, the whole thing. If I get caught up with that, my heart starts to race, I get anxious, I get irritable. I get caught up in the drama and then I feel like I've failed, that I'm bad at my job and I get exhausted. There is a cost.
>
> (Liv, early years TA)

Remember, the run-up to inspection is not the time for a self-improvement plan! This is a time of stress – adrenaline and cortisol of the threat system will be readily available. So you need to make a conscious effort to include things in your day you know help your health and well-being – for example, going out for a short walk every day, cooking a healthy meal or making sure you've got healthy food at home so you don't feel tempted to snack on junk. This is not the time to take up a new diet or exercise regime! Keep it simple and manageable: have a bath, go for a run, listen to some music. Keep your goals do-able.

This may seem very simple but what are the consequences of not doing this? In Chapter 2 we discussed the driven doing mode and mindful being mode and in Chapter 3 we looked at the system of emotional regulation. The trick is to recognise when you are in driven doing mode or the threat system and do something that will put you more in the mindful being mode or the soothing mode, to be present. This doesn't need to take a lot of time but can make all the difference. John, a secondary school teacher, says that when he's not present: 'I'm not all there, I'm irritable. I'm grasping, holding on to things and don't see things clearly. When I do this, I become inefficient, make mistakes. That bleeds into the next task and that can cause stress.'

You don't want to run out of all your resources before an inspection. By becoming aware of yourself in this way, and using mindfulness to take care of yourself and make wise choices about your well-being, you can face the inspection in a better state.

Before inspection

Pacing resource

Another thing that can help is pacing.[3] There is a tendency in our culture towards boom or bust: when you feel great you can be tempted to take on too much, to overwork; and then when you can't sustain it, you go into bust where you feel listless and don't want to do anything. Pacing involves stopping *before* you get tired. So if you're working at the weekend or in the evening in preparation for an inspection, then instead of trying to do, say, two hours straight, stop after half an hour and have a short break. This is where the mindfulness for transitions practices you learnt in Chapter 2 really come in handy. They don't take long, but they will refresh you and you'll be able to face the next half hour with more focus.

Notice how long it is before you feel tired and aim to stop before that point and have a breather. Once you're aware of how long that is, you can set a timer to go off at these intervals to remind you, and then you can do a short mindfulness practice or get up to have a stretch.

---

3   V. Burch and D. Penman, *Mindfulness for Health: A Practical Guide to Relieving Pain, Reducing Stress and Restoring Wellbeing* (London: Piatkus Press, 2013).

Task	How long until I felt tired/lost focus	Optimum time to stop before getting tired	What did I do in the breather? How was it?
For example, marking	45 minutes	30 minutes	Took 5 minutes, had a stretch and took a few conscious breaths. Feel refreshed and back on it!

During the inspection

Accept that this is going to be a stressful time. Everything discussed in the previous section still applies, but pay particular attention to the transitions and take a mindful moment in between them. This will stand you in good stead. You can also practise the three-step breathing space when something difficult happens, or you feel particularly stressed or overwhelmed.

Sam, a junior school teacher, had already started practising mindfulness when his school received notice of inspection:

We were given three weeks' notice. Two weeks in, someone said to me, 'Why are you so calm?' And then as we got nearer the inspection, time seemed to compress and I wasn't doing formal mindfulness practices but still trying to be mindful every day. And then the inspection came and just went.

Don't be surprised if you completely forget about mindfulness practices during the inspection. I was teaching a head teacher on a mindfulness course who had an inspection during the course. She said it went completely out of her mind during the inspection week. But because she was looking after herself in the run-up to the inspection and mindfulness practices were helping her sleep better, she felt resourced and refreshed for the inspection. I had another group of teachers who attended a mindfulness session the week of their inspection. They ran in and one of them said, 'I couldn't wait to come'.

During the inspection

Think about all the things that you do to keep yourself well. Jot them down. When you've completed a work task, make sure you complete one of your well-being priorities too. They are just as important.

My well-being list: five things I know will keep me well	Tick when done
1	
2	
3	
4	
5	

Remember, this will be a stressful time for everyone, so if a manager or colleague utters a cross or cutting word, try not to take it personally. Remember that most people will be in the red threat circle, trying to survive. I had a manager who was quite short and snappy with me during an inspection. I reflected that she was normally considerate in her communication, so this wasn't particularly directed at me. Forgive others and be friendly. It'll soon be over!

After the inspection

It's time to make a transition and let go. Accept that it might take a while for the adrenaline and cortisol to drop out of your system. It's time to 'rest and digest', and to put a couple of things in your diary for the weekend that feel like treats. However, you might need to adjust your expectations; my colleague's husband booked them into a luxury hotel with spa and pool following an inspection. She never made it to the spa and pool as she spent all weekend sleeping.

You can consciously enter that soothing (green) circle by letting yourself potter around in your pyjamas, with no particular agenda. Allow yourself to rest, or relax with music or a book. Cuddle up with your family or your pet on the sofa and watch a movie. Or meet a friend for coffee or lunch. All this will stimulate connection and oxytocin, which counteracts the stress hormones.

Mindfulness exercises to try

When you are stressed and busy, it might be too much to expect yourself to sit in meditation. You can feel fidgety and jangly and give up easily as you can't see the point. Some people find practising mindfulness with movement much easier at these times. By engaging in gentle stretching and breathing, they find their minds focus and settle far more easily. Try it and see!

Mile track practice

If your school has a mile track, try and get out on it once a day.

- Notice at what pace your body wants to walk and if this changes during the walk.

- Notice your breathing – fast or slow?

- Feel the temperature of the breath – cool from the air or warm.

- Take in the sights as you go round – trees, traffic, children and the changing perspective.

- Notice the sounds as you go – birds singing, traffic noise, shouts of children playing.

- It's possible to do this with a colleague, but make a golden rule of not talking about work for the duration! Take a break from it.

- At the end, spend a moment tuning in to your breathing and mood once more.

- How are you doing?

Mindful movement sequence

Movement is another laboratory in which you can explore mindfulness and it can be easier to focus as you are aligning your awareness with tangible sensations. Here are a few short sequences. You may want to do one after another if you are enjoying them and they seem to be having a positive effect.[4]

Sequence 1: these are smaller movements that can be done when you wake up or before you go to bed. Or when you want to bring a quiet, gentle focus to the day.

Movement 1: Opening palms

- Sit or lie down with your hands resting on your thighs and the palms facing upwards.

- Start with any one hand, bring your fingers together so that the pads of the fingers are bunched together.

- Open the fingers back out again so that they are spread.

- Be curious about the sensations:

   - The touch and texture of the pads of the fingers coming together.

   - The warmth or the pulse in the tips of the fingers.

   - The sensation of air as the fingers move away from each other and the palm opens up once more.

- If you like, you can sync the breath up with the movement, breathing in as the fingers come together and out as the palms open.

---

4   Note: All these movements are suggestions, but you are the expert of your own body. Please take care and if anything doesn't feel right, then either stop or adapt the movement. You may have some exercises of your own from a physio you can do instead. Whichever movement/ stretches you do, it is intended to be gentle. With mindful movement, we talk about working to the s*oft edge of the pose.* There should be an edge, a gentle stretch, but notice if you are striving to stretch or gritting your teeth – this would be a hard edge. There should be nothing like pain, so stop immediately if there is.

■ If this feels too complicated, don't worry – the breath will find its own rhythm.

■ Pause, notice if there is a difference in sensation now between the hand/fingers you have just moved. Maybe there is/isn't; just take notice.

■ Switch to the other hand and repeat the sequence. Notice the sensations in this hand.

■ Then, if you like, do both hands together.

■ Notice what feels good for you, if moving just one hand feels better then go back to that.

■ You can experiment with the pace of the movement, making it faster or slower to see how that feels.

■ Your eyes can be open or closed.

■ Spend a moment at the end, tuning in, noticing how you feel now.

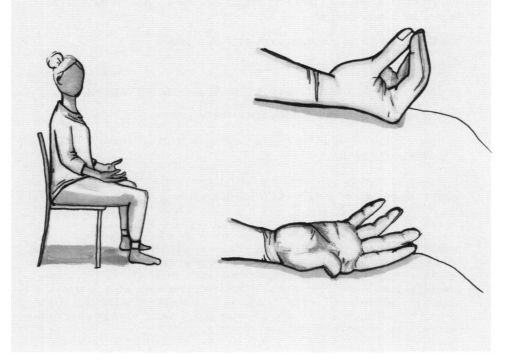

Movement 2: Sliding feet

▤ Sit on a chair so that your bottom is balanced but secure on the edge of the chair.

▤ If your chair is on a carpet you may want to have bare feet or for a wood/tiled floor you may want to wear socks.

▤ Hold the sides of the chair too, to offer support. Experiment with how tight your grip is and see what feels comfortable.

▤ Slide the sole of one foot away from you; notice how far it wants to go.

▤ Then slide it back.

▤ Tune in to the sensations:

  ▤ The contact of the foot gliding away, the sound, the temperature.

  ▤ Is it getting warmer or changing with the friction with the friction of the floor?

  ▤ Experience how you're not just moving the foot but engaging the muscle of the whole: the shin, thigh, bottom and lower back being engaged too.

▤ Pause and notice any difference in sensations between the foot/leg you have just moved and the other.

▤ Then switch to the other side, repeating the movement with the other foot.

▤ One leg might feel stiffer or easier.

▤ If you wish, you can do both feet together and see what that feels like.

▤ Spend a moment at the end, tuning in: what's here now?

Gentle stretching
(can be done in a chair too)

▨ Stand with feet hip width apart, feet firmly planted on the floor.

▨ Close your eyes and tune in to your internal weather. How are you doing just now?

▨ With eyes open or closed, gently float the arms up as if they are light as feathers.

▨ Stop when both arms are above the head, palms of hands facing parallel to each other.

▨ Breathe into the stretch – remember the soft edge of the pose.

▨ You may find that as you're breathing, the stretch naturally extends from your feet into your fingertips.

▨ Stay for a few moments and then bring the arms down as slowly as you can, as if moving through treacle. Savour the movement.

▨ Allow the arms to hang by the sides of the body and notice any sensations, particularly in the hands and fingertips.

▨ Repeat if enjoyable.

Opening to the sky and earth
(can be done in a chair or standing)

- Bring the palms to rest on the heart area, in front of the sternum between breasts or pecs.

- Gently rock the body – this immediately activates the parasympathetic nervous system.

- Smile – when we smile we release oxytocin and feel safe.

- Take a breath in. Lift one arm up over the head and reach the palm outwards as if reaching for an apple from a tree. Breathe out.

- Have the other hand stretched down the side of the body, with palm facing towards the earth.

- Stretch between these two points – take a deep breath in and out.

- Bring hands back to heart and swap arms so the other one reaches up now and the other one down.

- Take a deep breath in and out and bring hands back to centre.

- Repeat as many times as feels enjoyable.

- Finish with hands on heart again, a gentle rock and a smile.

Mindful walking

When going for a regular walk such as with the dog, choose to slow a section of the walk down. Take the time to appreciate the sights, sounds and smells of the environment you are in. Feel the contact your feet make with the ground and look up at the sky, noticing the clouds. Enjoy the faces of fellow walkers or the sight of pets sniffing around or running triumphantly.

What did you notice?

Why does this matter?

People think of practising mindfulness as sitting still in meditation. But if mindfulness is becoming present to whatever is happening in the moment, you can practise it sitting, walking, standing or lying down. Movement is just an effective way to develop mindfulness if you become aware and present to what you are doing. These movements are deceptively simple, but by engaging with them in this way, being present with them can be rich and satisfying. The movement provides a tangible focus and some people find it much easier to stay with the sensations of the movement and breathe while moving. It also has the added benefit of releasing any adrenaline and cortisol that can be racing around your system. Gentle stretching is a really simple way to feel energised. Everyone is different and this handbook provides a toolkit of practices so you can select and use the ones that work for you.

In this chapter, we've discussed:

▓ How in very stressful situations like an inspection you can look after yourself and keep your head clear.

▓ The exhaustion funnel and the tendency to overwork during stressful situations and the potential cost to this.

▓ Different mindful strategies to use before, during and after an inspection to help you be at your best.

▓ How mindfulness is not about sitting still but bringing it into all aspects of your life including moving and walking.

Chapter 5
Working with Thoughts and Overthinking

What is the consequence of not paying attention to our bodily sensations, feelings and thoughts? Our minds get into a mess, and we then create a mess that subsequently takes time to clear up.

Have you ever had the feeling of being so stressed that you feel that there is a piece of glass between you and the outside world? Beyond the glass are the other people, seeming to enjoy life – and there you are on the other side, feeling frozen and miserable. Or that sense of a snowball rolling towards you: you try to run, but as you do the snowball is getting bigger and gaining more momentum towards you. You feel totally overwhelmed. It's horrible to feel like that in either scenario, but if you are feeling like this or something similar, it is also clear that you have lost perspective, lost your footing and need to get on an even keel again. Let's take a closer look at this using the stress cycle:[1]

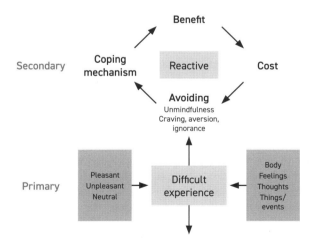

The stress cycle

---

1   Stress Cycle, Mindfulness in Action MBCT for stress coursebook.

Bring to mind a difficult experience: it could be physical, emotional, a difficult thought, or a challenging situation or colleague. You don't have to look very far to encounter difficulty in life; it's part of our everyday experience! This kind of stress and difficulty that comes from outside and is unlooked for and unwanted is called a primary difficulty. A primary difficulty means we didn't create it; it's come out of nowhere and it's totally outside our control. In other words it's the higher teaching of 'Shit happens'!

Primary difficulties are unavoidable, they happen to us all and in a way they connect us as human beings. None of us want to suffer and we all want to live in ease. So what's interesting here is what you do with them. If you're not aware, particularly to bodily sensations and how you're interpreting them, then it's quite easy to get into avoiding. Avoiding may have connotations for you of burying your head in the sand, but avoiding can also be quite active. It's not wanting something and pushing it away – in other words, reacting.

As with reacting and autopilot, you do what you have always done and go into a coping mechanism you have developed for this exact situation. It might be your coping mechanism is to blame someone else. There's a short-term benefit to this, as you may feel vindicated (*'It's not my fault!'*) and perhaps on the moral high ground. But blaming tends to lead to increasing thoughts and feelings of anger, resentment and contraction, which won't help you in the long run. There is a cost, so you go round the cycle again.

Or you might feel irritated and frustrated with someone at home and you shout at them. Again, there's a short-term benefit to this – you're getting it off your chest and letting them know how you feel! But what if they shout back? Then you're into a full-blown argument: you now have two problems, the thing that was originally annoying you and now the argument with all its repercussions.

The other common tendency is to blame yourself. You think, 'If only I'd foreseen this. If I only I'd been smarter/more organised/tougher,' and so on. You withdraw and become quiet, but your mind is a cacophony of harsh self-talk and criticism.

Overthinking and rumination are common habits here. You have a problem and your coping mechanism is that you are going to fix it and figure it out. This has a short-term benefit of feeling like you're doing something, that you're in control. But what if the problem can't be fixed just like that? That's when the tendency to ruminate, to go round and round and round in your head kicks in. You start thinking and analysing the thinking, or lose the tail of what you were trying to think about in the first place. The result is exhaustion; as one teacher said to me, 'I would burn my brain out'. Overthinking and rumination mean that you build a world, and then you fight it.

These examples of avoidance are called secondary difficulties because it's what you add to the existing difficulty. It's like rubbing salt in a wound. When you avoid, you bring tension to an already challenging situation and make it worse for yourself. So, what to do?

The good news is that becoming mindful can break the cycle at any point, even if you feel your mind and thoughts have already spun out of control. You can create that gap in the cycle by using mindful practices, such as grounding. When you're overthinking and ruminating, the energy in the body can frequently be located in the torso and the face. So by dropping your attention to your feet and the connection with the ground, that can really help.

Nobody is saying that you have to like the difficulty, but you can acknowledge it's there, rather than avoiding it. You can create some space around it, so that you identify with it less. That means that the issue is no longer dominating you; you can see that it's not you. It's a difficulty or a problem that has arisen and will abide and then pass away in its own time, as all things do. In this way, you become a bigger container for all the thoughts and feelings that will arise.

By engaging in this way, you are starting to bring perspective to your experience. You are no longer consumed by the issue but can see it for what it is – tightness or tension in the body, an unpleasant thought, feelings of hurt and disappointment – and acknowledge it rather than buying into it. You can see how you are *relating* to it. In this way, you can learn to bring *wise attention* to your experience, rather than *unwise attention.*

This is perfectly expressed by Rumi's poem 'The Guest House'.[2]

---

2   C. Barks, *The Essential Rumi* (New York: HarperCollins, 1995).

The Guest House

This being human is a guest house.
Every morning a new arrival.

A joy, a depression, a meanness,
some momentary awareness comes
as an unexpected visitor.

Welcome and entertain them all!
Even if they're a crowd of sorrows,
who violently sweep your house
empty of its furniture,
still, treat each guest honorably.
He may be clearing you out
for some new delight.

The dark thought, the shame, the malice,
meet them at the door laughing,
and invite them in.

Be grateful for whoever comes,
because each has been sent
as a guide from beyond.

Rumi

The ideas in this poem are inspiring and liberating. And they can be quite hard to actualise in the moment. But the opposite to this guest house owner is Basil Fawlty of *Fawlty Towers*. He can't accept the guests in his hotel, he doesn't like them, he doesn't want them there, he wants different guests! But his coping mechanism is to employ the British stiff upper lip, grit his teeth and pretend it's all fine. In this way, he gets more and more uptight until he can't take it any longer and explodes! So you might not be at the level of Rumi's guest house owner, but if you're somewhere between that and Basil Fawlty, you're doing well!

Thoughts are not facts

The most common mistake is to believe your thoughts are facts – they're solid and true. It's important to state that thinking is a necessary function – we need to plan, arrange, analyse to make sense of our day and work. However, the difficulty comes when you are stressed and harsh, judgemental thoughts arise – such as, 'I'm no good at this!' or 'I should be able to cope'. When you are already distressed, these kinds of unpleasant and harsh thoughts cause you further pain, and you can believe them to be true, just because you think them. As Mark Williams puts it, 'Your thoughts have ceased to be your servant and have become your master, and a very harsh and unforgiving master at that.'[3]

Mindfulness exercises to try

The following exercise allows you to explore the nature of your thoughts in everyday experience:

---

3   Penman and Williams, *Finding Peace in a Frantic World*, p. 41.

Sounds and thoughts

- Sit quietly, making sure you are grounded by sensing into the points of contact.

- Take your awareness to sounds – any sounds that are arising in your environment. It could be traffic outside, people moving around your house, your tummy rumbling.

- You may be labelling the sounds. That's OK, but see if you can get behind the label of the sound. What's its pitch, tone, volume or frequency?

- Notice if you're having thoughts about the sounds, whether you like them or not, whether they should or shouldn't be happening.

- If this is happening, register it and come back to allowing the sounds just to arise, abide and pass away.

- In a relaxed and open way, see if you can notice the sounds as they come and go – not clinging on to one or avoiding the other.

- Now drop the focus on sounds and come back to your body and breath for a few moments.

- Then in the same way that you brought your awareness to sounds, bring your awareness to thoughts.

- Thoughts can be quite shy. As soon as you turn your awareness to them they can scuttle away! Don't worry if this is one time your thoughts are absent.

- Just as you approached sound, allow thoughts to arise in their own way.

- Perhaps you've already been swept off by your thoughts – that's OK. Come back to that broader sense of awareness and start again.

- You might notice the texture of thoughts – dark and sticky or light and fluffy. You may be wanting to pursue one thought and push away another. Remember this is normal, it's what we do as human beings.

- Reflect that thoughts are just like sounds – phenomena that arise, abide and then pass away in their own time. You don't need to manage or fix them.

- Bring the meditation to a close by focusing on the body and breath once more.

Why this matters

In mindfulness, thoughts are events that occur in the mind. They may be regurgitated thoughts that we've had before, or memories, or influenced by what we've seen in the media, or even dream-like. They are just mental events and are like the other sense impressions: sound, light, smell, taste. They will arise, abide and pass away like clouds in the sky, or a leaf carried by the current of a river. You don't need to get involved with them and you certainly don't need to believe them. You wouldn't relate to a sound in that kind of way. You can create some distance from thoughts, they're not inherently you or yours.

Learning to work with difficulty so that you don't avoid it but don't become overwhelmed is a skill. It takes practice and time as we all have our own reactive coping mechanisms. A common coping mechanism is overthinking or ruminating instead of allowing what is happening. No human being wants difficulty so working in this way will feel counterintuitive. One way to think about it is not 'adding more fuel to the fire'. The primary difficulty is enough on its own – if you let your mind run amok with it then you will cause yourself further tension and distress.

Meditation: approaching rather than avoiding

Find a quiet space where you can sit and won't be disturbed.

- Make sure you are comfortable, fully supported, with hands resting on legs or on a cushion for support.

- Spend a few minutes tuning in with the points of contact with the seat and the feet. The bottom and lower back on the chair, the contact with the earth.

- Explore these sensations, getting underneath the label of 'feet on floor' and sensing what's actually there: Contact? Pressure? Texture of socks or clothing?

- It's really important in this exercise to be grounded, so spend as long as you need to feel a sense of stability or being solid. This will bring its own balance and help you feel more steady.

- Now take the attention to the breath. Let the breath naturally come and go, again really tuning in to the sensations, the rise and the fall of the body with the breath.

- You might want to put a hand on where you're feeling the breath in the upper body, on the belly or the chest. Feel the gentle contact and pressure as the upper body fills on the in breath and falls back on the out breath. Let the breath soothe you. Take as long as you need to establish a sense of calm and peace, however small.

- Now bring to mind something that's challenging. Make it mild: an irritation, a snappy word spoken, or a feeling of impatience you've encountered recently. Maybe something's happened today at school, or on the commute or at home. A mild example is all you need to work with at the moment.

- Notice what's happening in the body when you bring this to mind. Is there tightness or tension somewhere? Contraction or holding the breath? Scan the body for sensations.

- Maybe you've gone immediately into thinking. Thoughts like, 'They shouldn't have done that!' or 'Why does this always happen to me?' Notice this.

- Thoughts are usually mirrored in the body, so scan the body and notice any tightness, tension or holding.

- This is what we call approaching. You can imagine breathing into the tightness and tension in the body and softening it with an out breath, releasing it.

- If you find yourself going into thinking again, repeat the process of scanning the body for tightness and tension and softening it with the breath.

- In this way you're allowing and acknowledging what is happening for you right now, mentally, physically and emotionally.

- If any of this feels overwhelming at all, return to the stability of the contact of the feet on the floor, bottom on the chair, hands on the legs. Explore the sensations here and use the breath to soothe you. You need to go at your own pace and doing these steps will bring stability, help create a bigger container.

- Now drop any reflections and come back to feet on floor, bottom on chair, breathing. Give yourself a few minutes to settle and arrive back in the room.

What did you notice?

_____

_____

_____

_____

_____

Why does this matter?

Life can be inherently challenging – it's not you getting it wrong. Difficulties come and go just like happiness comes and goes – they are two sides of the same coin. However, what you do with this is important – do you react and make things worse? Or can you create perspective by acknowledging the difficulty but not getting bound up in it? In this way, you can depersonalise the experience. It's not you trapped on one side of the glass and other people having a nice life on the other side. These reflections will help connect you with what it means to be part of the human race.

In this chapter, we've looked at:

- The difference between primary and secondary difficulty.

- How when you react and avoid what is happening, this can add to your distress.

- How rumination and overthinking lead to you becoming further entangled. However, there is a way of approaching difficulty that leads to greater clarity and perspective.

- The notion that thoughts are not facts. They are like sounds – they arise, abide and pass away in their own time. You don't need to become involved with them.

- How this is a challenging practice, it goes against the grain, but by building these skills you are becoming a bigger container and more resilient.

When you approach rather than avoid, you become more flexible. Like a reed in the wind, you may bend with it but you don't snap. You calmly wait for the wind to drop or change direction.

Chapter 6
Mindfulness for Stressful Times

For an Observation

An observation, a work scrutiny, learning walks and drop-ins to classroom, more than an inspection, are snapshots. It's a moment in time, a glance into your teaching; it can never tell the whole story. However, a lot can rest on it so it's no wonder that it's stressful. You can be a confident teacher, know your subject really well, have great relationships in the classroom. But as soon as someone comes into your classroom 'to observe' or to scrutinise or moderate your books, you can feel anxious and nervous.

Why is this? Put simply, you feel judged, personally and professionally, and are put on the spot. And any judgement, or even implied judgement, can feel like a threat, real or perceived. This will fire up your amygdala, the oldest part of your brain that is to do with survival, and send your nervous system into fight, flight and freeze mode.

'What if they think I am a rubbish teacher?' 'What if so-and-so doesn't behave?' As we discussed in the previous chapter, you can believe these thoughts to be true and that leads to further stress. Also, these thoughts are triggering a signal to your nervous system to go into the threat zone.

Adrenaline and cortisol will start to flood your system. Your heart might race, you may feel suddenly hot and sweaty, tongue-tied, or freeze just when you need to be at your best. These physical symptoms go along with feeling irritable, jangled and reactive. So how can mindfulness help you manage this?

In Chapter 4, we discussed the importance of paying attention to bodily sensations because the body gives you signals about what is happening, long before your mind catches up. The ability to fight, flee or freeze is mainly a physical phenomenon, as illustrated by the physical symptoms above. Your heart races to pump blood around the body, oxygenating the muscles to enable you to fight or run. You sweat to cool down the muscles so that you're able to move faster; your throat might constrict, because what good is talking to a sabre-toothed tiger? Also, you may suddenly feel like you need to use the loo, because the body is getting rid of any excess to allow it to be lighter and travel quicker.

Going back to the threat circle in Chapter 3, you're not doing this because there is something wrong with you or you're stupid. This is how we as a species have survived over thousands of years. A humorous way of putting it is that our ancestors were a race of 'worriers' rather than 'warriors'. But these survival tactics are not appropriate to the situation – none of these skills of fighting, fleeing, freezing or overthinking are going to help you in this situation.

This applies across the board, no matter what role you might have in a school or college. Sue had taught at the same secondary school for 18 years and had been head of department for a number of years. But she wasn't exempt from the kind of stress observations and work scrutiny provided:

> I was struggling professionally with observations. When lesson observations came about, I was a mess, I couldn't perform. I couldn't even plan for the lessons as I would overplan. I would be three weeks planning for one session and still couldn't think clearly about what they wanted me to do. I was crippled by the stress.
>
> (Sue, head of department at a secondary school)

Going back to the stress cycle in Chapter 5, once you are in the threat mode, the negativity bias is operating. The negativity bias is the capacity to see everything as a potential threat and narrow your focus on it, rather than having a broader view. You may lose focus or adopt overplanning as your short-term coping strategy, which means you get into a state where you've lost perspective. Being in the threat zone is exhausting, and tiredness can further add to low mood, eroding your confidence about your ability to do this.

If this is happening, you need to activate your parasympathetic nervous system to calm down and counteract fight, flight and freeze. Any of the practices you've done so far in this book will help with this, for example the mindful minute, the emotional barometer, the three-step breathing space in the moment. And the mindful movement, body scan when you have a bit more time. Once you do these, you create a bit of space and room for perspective. From here, you have a choice: do you want to continue thinking/acting in this reactive, driven mode? Is it helping? If not then you can make a choice of what to do. You can use a mindfulness practice to bridge between a more driven, reactive mode and a state of mind that is calmer and more purposeful. Mindfulness helps you get the initiative back.

Mindfulness exercise to try

If we're feeling stuck, or paralysed by nerves, it's very difficult in the moment to know what to do for ourselves. This is where the breathing space with action step is really useful.

Breathing space with action step

- Stand or sit. Have your eyes open or closed. Feel the floor beneath your feet.

- Scan for a sense of internal weather/mood. Say hello to whatever's there without changing or fixing it.

- Now focus your attention exclusively on the breath, the in-breath and the out-breath. Feel the rhythm of the breath as it comes and goes.

- Now broaden back out to the whole of you sitting or standing here.

- Pop in the question to yourself, 'How can I best take care of myself right now?'

- Be patient and see what comes.

- Then make sure you do it – however small, silly or counterintuitive it seems.

What did you notice?

_____

_____

_____

_____

_____

Why is this important?

Once you've taken that first step, you're stepping away from the stress cycle and auto-pilot and stepping into a more creative and confident mindset. This exercise can be performed in the run-up to an observation or afterwards.

> I started to see what part my behaviour was playing with this thing. It came at a time where I needed that reflection space, of how my bodily sensations were causing me to have physical sensations of anxiety. Looking back, there were ridiculous things happening in the classroom such as my ears popping. I went to the doctor and there was no reason for it. I was feeling dizzy. Then I realised, looking at the stress cycle, that I wasn't taking deep enough breaths. My heart was palpitating and that was making me think I was ill and that was happening regularly in lessons, thinking about being observed.
>
> (Sue, head of department at a secondary school)

The mind: like Velcro for bad experiences and Teflon for good ones

The psychologist Rick Hanson describes the negativity bias as the mind being like Velcro for bad experiences and Teflon for good ones.[1] Velcro is sticky and feels like it has more substance; Teflon, on the other hand, slides off us. And yet both are equally true – Velcro or Teflon thoughts or emotions are created in the same way, and arise, abide and pass away in their own time, as discussed in the last chapter. Think about the last time you had professional feedback of any kind – did you zone in on the critical/developmental comments and ignore the positive and encouraging ones, rather than take them both on equal level? Or consider the last time somebody paid you a compliment – did you let it become like Teflon and deflect and say 'Oh, that was nothing'?

Mindfulness in decision-making

When you are stressed or driven, you lose efficiency, and although your body may feel energised, your mind might feel foggy and you find it hard to focus. Making a decision about what to prioritise for an observation can be particularly elusive.

After practising mindfulness for some weeks, Sandra realised:

> I'm kind of a gut instinct person. That can be good but it's so easy to think, I need to decide on this now so I can move on to something else.

This is the difficulty with a problem. It feels uncomfortable and you want to get rid of it. However, by trying to problem-solve prematurely, you can make poor decisions.

---

1   Rick Hanson, *Buddha Brain: The Practical Neuroscience of Happiness, Love and Wisdom* (Oakland: New Harbinger Press, 2009).

Mindfulness exercise to try

Unhooking

- Sit or stand comfortably.

- Bring to mind the problem or the difficulty. This may show up as a thought or an image.

- Unhook from that thought or image and take your attention directly to the body.

- What do you notice? Tightness, or tension? Feeling sick? Heaviness?

- Whatever is there, allow it and breath some tender, soothing breaths into that area.

- If you find yourself going back up into the thoughts and images in your head, unhook again and come back to the direct sensations in the body and start the process once more.

- You might find that these sensations move and change; they don't stay static. They may ease or release, or they may disappear altogether!

What did you notice?

_____

_____

_____

_____

_____

Why this matters

Emotions aren't just a cognitive thing, they show up in the body too. When we feel overwhelmed, emotions can drive us to actions and impulses that might not be the best course of action. By learning to unhook from the powerful grip of thoughts and habits that are underpinned by strong emotions, you can create some space, some distance from the issue and come to see the issue afresh.

By becoming aware and _breathing with_ these emotions and discomfort, we are widening 'the window of tolerance', as Dr Dan Siegel puts it.[2] This grows our resilience but also our creativity.

One benefit of this is that by slowing down the process, you can come to recognise when something needs to be immediately prioritised or whether you can allow it more time.

---

2   D. J. Siegel, _The Developing Mind, 3rd edition_ (New York: Guilford Press, 2020).

Surviving and thriving in an observation/learning walk/ work scrutiny

Staying grounded is really helpful to manage stress and nerves in the run up to an observation or for decompressing after one. When you're anxious, stressed and caught up with the thoughts in your head, you need a way of becoming grounded and bringing the energy back down into the body. It's like a boat being tossed at sea – if you can drop an anchor then you will feel more stable. You may still be rocked by the tide, but there will something solid there, keeping you moored.

Before the observation, spending some time focusing on your lower body is a great way of getting out of your head and the cacophony of thoughts. The grounding practice is an effective way to do this.

Grounding practice

- Sit in a seat in which you are comfortable, making sure your upper body is alert and awake but supported as well.

- If you can have your legs uncrossed and your feet directly on the floor, this helps to activate the parasympathetic nervous system.

- Take a few breaths to arrive and have a sense of the shape of the body.

- Tune in to sounds for a moment, to have an awareness of your environment. Eyes can be open or closed.

- Now direct your awareness to your feet, particularly the contact the feet are making with the floor. What does it feel like? What direct sensations can you notice?

- Pressure?

- The texture of your shoe or sock against your skin?

- Temperature – coolness or warmth?

- Perhaps the toes are bunched together or spread out?

- Take a few moments to explore the sensations in the feet.

- Your mind may wander off, which is inevitable, so as soon as you notice that it has, gently guide it back to the feet without any sense of giving yourself a hard time.

- Then move your awareness from the feet and up the legs. If it helps you could use the image of a torch, shining a light on different parts as it goes.

- The tiny bones of the ankles.

- The lower legs, with the bony shin in front and the soft calf muscle behind.

- The thighs – the biggest muscles and bones in the body, the backs of the thighs making contact with the chair.

- Finally, the bottom; you may feel your sit bones – the bones making contact with the seat – balancing your weight on the seat. Again, really explore the sensations of the bum on the chair – what can you notice?

- Is it hard or soft? Comfortable or uncomfortable? Again, just noting without any need to do anything about it.

- Then bring your awareness to the front of the pelvis and start to tune in to sensations of breathing here.

- The breath can sometimes feel like the tide, swelling and subsiding. If you'd like to, you can put a hand here to really tune in to those sensations of breath in this area.

- You've grounded your awareness in the lower body; you may even find you are enjoying the gentle rock of the breath in this area, like a boat in harbour.

What did you notice?

_____

_____

_____

_____

_____

During an observation/learning walk/work scrutiny:

- Remember to feel your feet on the floor and take a few conscious breaths every so often.

- If you are having physical signs of stress, this will soothe them.

⬛ Even if you aren't, it will keep you grounded, purposeful and able to perform and communicate.

After the observation/learning walk/ work scrutiny

Practise active listening during the feedback and be genuinely curious. Don't be afraid to probe for more detail if it's not clear, and ask for specific examples. Remember, you do have initiative here! Take in the positive points as well as the developmental ones (all effective feedback should have both). Don't let the positive feedback be like Teflon and don't let the negative feedback attach itself like Velcro! Remember, they are both equal points about your teaching/work. So remember to soak in the good points rather than dismiss them in favour of the critical points.

Why this matters

Situations such as lesson observations may immediately fire up our sympathetic nervous system and mean we are not performing at our best when we need to. Exercises such as the breathing space with action step can help you keep the initiative and be more purposeful. Practising mindfulness in the run-up to an observation may mean you are more in the moment and less caught up in your head and therefore reactive during it. The grounding practice is a great way to settle yourself before, or decompress after, an observation. The purposefulness that mindfulness can give you means you can actively be part of the feedback process, being genuinely curious and probing when you need more clarity but also taking in and enjoying the positive comments!

In this chapter, we've discussed:

⬛ How to manage the very real stress of observations/learning walks/work scrutiny.

⬛ The negativity bias: how the mind is like Velcro for negative experiences and Teflon for positive ones.

⬛ When events trigger a 'threat response' in our nervous system and how to activate the parasympathetic nervous system to counteract fight, flight and freeze.

- How to keep the initiative, especially in the feedback process, and not being too quick to dismiss your qualities in favour of hearing about your faults.

Chapter 7

Mindfulness for Stressful Times

Difficult Communication with a Colleague/Manager or Parent

'Hell is other people,' the philosopher Jean Paul Sartre declared in his play *Huis Clos.*[1]

It's certainly true that, at times, living and working with our families, colleagues and friends demands patience. When communication is smooth, you feel you're in a flow of activity, but when it's going badly it can feel like stepping out onto a minefield. Communication is bound to be difficult at times, no matter who we are and who we are conversing with. It's an inevitable part of life. So how can mindfulness help you actively listen, become aware of your emotional triggers and read between the lines?

Word of caution: if you feel that you are being bullied or harassed in work, it's crucial that you don't suffer in silence. Speak out and seek support from colleagues/friends, your union or mediation services. Even if it is a misunderstanding, you are taking the first step to resolving it. This will help you feel empowered rather than powerless.

Jen came back from maternity leave to find that there'd been a significant change of management at her school. She'd missed out on lots of new developments during that time and felt that nobody had taken that into consideration. She was just expected to catch up. Added to this, she'd returned from maternity leave early due to personal issues, and felt that she needed some support and understanding around this.

---

1   J. P. Sartre, *Huis Clos and Other Plays* (London: Penguin Classics, 2000).

I came back so soon, and then I couldn't work out whether the problems I was experiencing back in school were down to post-natal depression or some work-related stress. It soon became too much and I had two weeks off work, which is when I realised that it was work-related stress. I needed to put something in place; I didn't want to be on anti-depressants my whole life.

(Jen, secondary school teacher)

Jen was already in a vulnerable state coming back to school. As you know, schools are busy environments and rightly or wrongly don't always take an individual's needs into account. The result of all the changes, the lack of awareness of her as an individual and the expectation that Jen would just 'get on with it' meant that it was causing her to have poorer mental health than before she returned and left her feeling isolated.

It's easy for difficulties in communication to snowball and get out of hand. In my work room, a colleague was finding communication difficult with a new manager. There had been changes to the subject area and this colleague had health issues and no doubt needed more support in how to manage this. However, the situation quickly escalated. Nearly every email this manager sent, my colleague would react. Even when we re-read the emails and reassured her there was nothing untoward, she felt disconnected with the individual and didn't trust her. These angry outbursts were further affecting her health, leaving her feeling drained and helpless.

So how can mindfulness help resolve difficulties in communication? How can you respond, not react?

When you are reacting, you are in the threat zone (see Chapter 3). This doesn't just affect your body but colours your thoughts and emotions too. It affects your perception (remember the negativity bias in Chapter 6). You can hang on to that which you perceive as negative and make more of it than there is. And you can ignore any positive or more neutral elements that contradict or modify this view. It can go round and round in your head. In the absence of more information, the mind will start to fill in the gaps and fix a storyline. You start to speculate and soon become convinced that your speculations are accurate, looking for signs to confirm your hypothesis. Or you misjudge a situation but carry on down a trajectory as if your judgement were true. In other words, you build a world and then you fight it out.

How can mindfulness help us unravel some of these patterns and stories, so that you can see clearly and take appropriate action? Taking that moment, creating space with mindfulness practice is always helpful, because it puts you on a more even keel.

I have found the ideas of nonviolent communication (NVC) very helpful in better under-standing my responses and the motivations of others around me.[2] NVC is about listening deeply to the needs of others and your own needs. Needs in NVC aren't personal, they're human values that connect us all, such as the need for safety, for love and affection, for respect. Practising NVC means you can honour yourself while developing com-passion for the other; it's not a either/or situation. You realise that everyone is trying to be happy, well and safe, but the way they communicate this might be confusing or even irritating. By peeling back the meaning behind the words used, you can come to a deeper understanding of yourself and others, moment by moment. Everyone is trying to honour universal values and needs, every minute, every day. Mindfulness is a foundational quality to NVC as it involves awareness, seeing what connects us and developing the skills to honour this. These techniques can seem deceptively simple but in fact are powerfully transformative.

The ideas of NVC have been further developed by my colleague Simon McKibben,[3] who is an expert in NVC and mindfulness. The ability to be present is the foundational quality that underpins NVC. According to McKibben, the first step is GAP. We've already spoken about the importance of creating a gap – and in this context, GAP stands for 'grounded aware presence'.

As discussed in previous chapters, with conflict and difficulty, you need to give yourself some attention – use the grounding techniques you have learnt and become present to what is happening, physically, mentally and emotionally. The stress cycle in Chapter 5 showed you that when something unpleasant happens, you tend to *avoid it* – that is, try to push it away. This rarely works, as if you try and close the door then the unresolved feelings or emotions will find their way in through the window. Better to acknowledge what's happening for you and give it some space, remembering it's OK to feel hurt or a bit wounded by unpleasant communication – you are only human after all. But then it's what you do with that communication, how you interpret it. Are you causing *secondary difficulty* for yourself? You may need to give yourself some empathy – understanding and acknowledgement of your feelings and emotions, as if seeing them through the eyes of a loving friend, rather than harsh self-judgement. Once you have *paused for presence* and given yourself some *empathy*, then you are ready to return to the situa-tion once more.

Another of the aspects that's really helpful in NVC is that of observation. You can recall the incident/communication as it was, as if a video camera had recorded it and was playing it back. What was the setting, the body language, what was actually said? It may

---

2   M. B. Rosenberg, *Nonviolent Communication: A Language of Compassion* (Encinitas: Puddledancer Press, 2001).

3   See https://www.living-presence.co.uk.

help to write it down. This is useful in stripping away your speculations and interpretations by focusing on what actually happened, rather than what you *think* happened. This helps with achieving a more rounded perspective on the situation at hand.

All this helps to establish GAP.

You are then in a position to *express* or *receive* with the person in question: expressing is communicating, receiving is listening. You need to express honestly how you found the exchange or communication. This might take some discernment on your part, depending on who you are talking to. But it's important to say what impact it had on you, without blaming anyone else. It might be that it touches on some core values you have, such as the need to be respected and valued – you are doing your best for the situation.

Then you need to receive empathically. Whether you are the person who has found the exchange difficult or you have said something that someone else has reacted to, connection is fundamental to rebuilding trust and stability. At this point you are listening, you are giving someone the benefit of the doubt and hearing what they actually said and why they said what they said. Or you could be hearing how what you have said has affected them.

Both the positions of expressing and receiving are positions of vulnerability – you are going beyond the need to be right, blame or control. This doesn't come easily, so notice if you've stopped listening and are focusing instead on formulating your answers back. *Pause for presence* regularly during the conversation. Pausing for presence needs only take a couple of seconds, checking in with how you are doing and picking up on any bodily sensations, such as tension and tightness. But it's important because it's so easy in these situations to go into autopilot and react. By doing this you get a handle on the bodily sensations that are giving you information about how you might be feeling, before they start to negatively affect your input into the conversation.

Remember, in a busy environment like a school, it's easy for things to come out the wrong way or be a bit blunter than you meant them. We have all done it. It's important not to take things too personally but at the same time address issues if there is a repeated pattern. Schools/colleges have a duty of care towards staff, but equally staff need to be pro-active, as falling into complaining and blame disempowers you. Remember that heads and managers are just people too, doing their best and trying to get it right. A head of a teaching union once told me that because of the perceived hierarchical structure in schools, school staff don't always take the opportunity to question or clarify motivations or decisions, which might lead to further misunderstandings or lack of a sense of agency.

GAP takes courage as it is a vulnerable space, but it's also an empowering one. To let go of blaming self or other, or the need to justify or defend yourself, you can enter into truly human communication with another. Any sailor will tell you that when a rope is sheared, the strongest place in the rope becomes where the knot is. Just as when you are grounded and present, can listen and express, then harm can be repaired and human communication can really flourish.

> Looking back, I was mismanaged. But mindfulness helped me reflect back and unpick it and make sense of it. I remember something I read in a book about the storytelling mind and I thought, 'That's what I've been doing'. I was so caught up in what others thought of me. The changes in behaviour through practising mindfulness started to have a massive effect on me and helped me to reflect and give myself space.
>
> (Jen, secondary school teacher)

Mindfulness exercises to try

50–50 awareness

When communicating with others, particularly if it's a difficult situation, the idea of 50-50 awareness is helpful. In short, 50-50 awareness is when half our awareness is inside ourselves and half our awareness is outside ourselves. You can practise this alone to start with to get a feel for it and then bring it into your everyday life

Sit quietly somewhere you won't be disturbed for a few minutes.

▦ Imagine a friend/colleague/family member is telling you something really important – they need your attention! Mimic how your body language would be.

▦ Now take stock – are you leaning forward to listen?

   ▦ Tensing your shoulders with no thought of your posture?

   ▦ Gripping your hands together?

   ▦ Another version of these?

Take a moment to experience, this is what it's like when your attention is 100% outside yourself.

Now imagine you're in a staff meeting that has dragged on. You're hot, tired and fed up. Someone that you know is a windbag brings up a point in any other business. You know you could be stuck there for another 20 minutes. Mimic your body language.

Are you:

▦ Leaning back in your seat?

▦ Rolling your eyes or have stopped making eye contact with the room?

▦ Looking at your phone underneath the table?

▦ Another variation of this?

This is what it's like when you withdraw your attention so it's 100% inwards. Now imagine what it would be like to have 50% of your attention on you and 50% on the other person. Adjust your posture accordingly.

▦ You can have an alert body while being relaxed, noticing bodily sensations as they arise.

▦ You can look after your own needs/posture while still giving someone your attention.

▦ You can work on the principle of 'just enough' energy and effort without straining forward or collapsing back.

▦ You can notice if you are formulating answers and drop back from this into listening once more.

Now you've tried this on your own, practise in real-life situations, if only for a few minutes. Build up this skill gradually – it will pay off!

What did you notice?

_____

_____

_____

_____

_____

Why this matters

When you're working in an unrelenting environment like a school or a college, it's so easy for awareness to be 100% outside yourself, focused on what's happening externally, people, pupils and situations. This isn't sustainable, so what happens is that you collapse into exhaustion and feel disconnected and withdraw. That's when your awareness becomes 100% internal as you brood or ruminate. These are two opposite poles that you can flip-flop between. But a healthy attitude is having 50% of your awareness on yourself and 50% of awareness externally. This affects everything, from your body language to your mood and the way you communicate. Practising having your awareness as 50–50 and frequently *pausing for presence* during the conversation, will help you feel steady, grounded and that you have more initiative in the conversation.

> At the end of the day you are in an organisation and the breadth of what you're doing and expected to do is so wide. There is a pending difficult conversation, I don't like conflict, I feel anxious around it. Afterwards I review it and think, did I do that right? Then I have negative self-talk, I'm not good enough. That's when focusing on the breath comes in really handy. I might have gone over and above to help a colleague and then they've come back at me with something uncalled for and I take it personally. I can reflect that person would have said it to anyone but I take it personally, which I try not to. That's when I become deregulated and really anxious. I do struggle with anxiety so then I need to shift my focus using the mindful breathing.
>
> (Tim, primary school head teacher)

When you're tired and had a long day, it can be quite difficult to figure out what your needs are. By laying them out in front you, something might spark your attention or resonate with you. Take a look at these, are there any that speak to you today?

Examples of different needs are:[4]

Autonomy – believing you have choice

Celebration – to praise yourself, a colleague, pupil or parent who is doing well

Integrity – authenticity, creativity, meaning and self-worth

Interdependence – appreciation, closeness, consideration, safety, empathy, honesty, warmth

---

4   Rosenberg, *Nonviolent Communication.*

Physical nurturance – fresh air, food, exercise, protection from disease, rest, shelter, water

Play – beauty, fun, harmony, inspiration, peace

What did you notice?

_____

_____

_____

_____

_____

Why this matters

Being in touch with your needs empowers you. It takes you out of the personal realm and helps you realise that this is what all humans need to thrive. It's not you being awkward, selfish or wanting your own way. By connecting with your need, you feel authentic: _Yes! That's what's going on_. There's a strength that comes from this clarity; you feel more on solid ground, and from there it's just a short step to express what you need or listen to what others need. You can put them on cards or Post-its somewhere where you can see them. Who knows, it might help others at work discover what they need too!

In this chapter, we've looked at:

▓ How mindfulness is a foundational quality for communication improvement skills like NVC.

▓ How GAP allows you to express yourself and listen to others skilfully.

▓ How by _pausing for presence_, you can stay grounded and calm during challenging communication and not tip into reacting or being defensive.

- How 50–50 awareness is a key resource in managing our own energy, particularly in communication, so we don't finish the school day feeling exhausted.

- How it's hard to distinguish what you need sometimes. Looking at an external list can you help pinpoint exactly what you need at this moment.

Chapter 8

Filling the Tank

Kindness and Self-Compassion

You don't go into teaching or working in a school/college and stay there for the money. School staff are, by nature, carers who put the nurturing of others – namely, young people and children – first. But schools/colleges are increasingly complex environments and have to meet many different needs. Approximately 25% of young people have a recognisable mental health disorder, with 10% needing specialist help. What's heartbreaking is that 50% of mental health issues are established by the age of 15 and 75% before the age of 25.[1] These are national averages; in the demographic you are working in, there may be more or less.

In your work situation, you may have a sense of an overwhelming need and not being able to fulfil it. Often, that can go along with feeling guilty or selfish for attending to your own needs and taking care of yourself. So how can you put something back into your own 'tank', so that you aren't running on empty and don't burn out?

> My role at the time was trying to fix things, and trying to fix things that couldn't easily be fixed. The message I was trying to put across to staff and to pupils was that we can work through things, we can find strategies. But in myself I was still in that fix mode, I was trying to do that fixing, even though I knew that I couldn't. It felt that was what I still needed to be aiming for.
>
> (Sarah, ALN-CO in secondary school)

The starting point for this is 50–50 awareness discussed in the last chapter. However complex the school is or its needs are, you are part of the mix. You need to bring yourself into the picture. Practising keeping 50% of your awareness on yourself – your posture, the way you move, your basic needs such as making sure that you eat/drink/go to the loo – will have a big effect even on a simple level. It might not always be possible to do things the moment you need to, but having this 50–50 attitude as your lodestone means

---

1   Mental Health Foundation, *Mental Health Statistics*.

that you will be able to maintain your energy and purpose, get less distracted and feel less frazzled at the end of the day.

Added to this, it is important to consider the *negative bias* here. We have already defined this as, 'The mind is like Velcro for bad experiences and Teflon for good ones'. As discussed, negative experiences tend to weigh heavier in your mind because you tend to perceive them as more 'true'. Therefore, you give them more focus and attention than positive ones, letting them slide off. But what you dwell on grows, and if you learn to give the same weight to positive experiences, really soaking them in and allowing them to affect you, then you will feel nourished.

Neuroscience has proved that rather than the brain being fixed, it has neuroplasticity.[2] The neurons in your brain are constantly shaping and being shaped by things such as thoughts, emotions, knowledge, other people and environment. And *neurons that wire together, fire together.*[3] In other words: the more you dwell on experiences positive or negative, the more these will affect how your brain functions and build stronger synaptic connections and neural pathways. In plain English, these synaptic connections are like highways in the brain; the more you travel down certain highways, the more they become the route of choice, your *go-to* place. You start travelling down them automatically, like you don't have to think about your travel route from work to home. But because of neuroplasticity, you can build new neural pathways, new brain highways and byways, that help you maintain a more balanced and healthy perspective. Mindfulness helps you build creative thinking and positive emotion.

> It gives you that awareness of a situation where you can step back and think 'Hang on, this isn't me being a crap teacher or disorganised or not being able to cope', because that's what used to come straight in my head. But actually now I realise, 'Hang on, a teacher's walked into my lesson, a child has thrown up in the corner, all of this – I've got to get this done'. It gives you that awareness that, 'No, this is an unusually difficult situation I'm in'. I give myself the time to stop, think and say 'Hold on a second, I'll be with you in 2 minutes', rather than feeling like I have to react immediately.
>
> (Sian, Healthy Schools co-ordinator, secondary school)

So you need to be less like Velcro for bad experiences, and more like Teflon for good ones. Going back to 50–50, I have emphasised the physical benefits but one affects the other. If you feel less tired and frazzled, that will affect your mood. You may be clearer

---

2   Weare and Bethune, *Implementing Mindfulness in Schools.*
3   D. O. Hebb, *The Organization of Behaviour: A Neuropsychological Theory* (New York: Wiley & Sons Inc., 1949).

and feel lighter and that allows you to make good choices for yourself. You will feel more nourished.

Self-care is not selfish

School staff can get into the habit of giving to others and then feel selfish or guilty if they take time for themselves. Even on mindfulness courses, the majority of educators will be motivated to come and learn for the benefit of their own learners. It's only after a few weeks they realise and comment, 'I really need this for myself!'

> Finding the time to practise mindfulness was tricky at the start and then I did carve out some time. I've always been the first one to get up in the morning, so I just got up a little bit earlier again and tried to build it into a routine. Come downstairs, put the kettle on and then go and sit. Then tea would be ready. Sometimes I'd come down and didn't feel like doing it or be really busy or restless, telling myself: 'I haven't got time for this'. But then it just takes a bit of commitment to say, 'No, I'm going to stop and take some time to do this'.
>
> (Paul, primary school teacher)

The work of Paul Gilbert and Professor Frances Marotos of the University of Derby shows that not only does the mind affect the body, but the body affects the mind.[4] Therefore, by paying attention to the outer – our body, facial expressions, voice and posture – this can deeply affect our inner mood, emotions, thoughts and attitudes. We will explore this in the next three exercises.

Regal walking

- Imagine yourself to be royal – a king or a queen.
- Adjust your posture accordingly so that it communicates your status and your dignity: shoulders back, chest open.
- Your back should have a gentle curve.
- Slow down – you are a royal and don't need to rush!
- Take calm and deliberate steps.
- Breathe deeply.
- How does that feel?

---

4   P. Gilbert and F. Marotos, *Compassionate Mind Training Manual* (Derby: University of Derby, 2021), pp. 25–26.

Playing a role

Research shows that the emotions we bring to mind influence not only what we think about but also how we approach different situations.[5]

Facial expression

We may not be conscious of them but our facial expressions, smiling or scowling, affect our mood. Let's play with this!

▓ Adopt a neutral facial expression.

▓ Now switch to a smiling face, like you are seeing a good friend or loved one.

▓ Take a moment to notice how this feels different – if it does.

▓ Switch back to the neutral facial expression.

▓ Then back to a smiling expression.

▓ Move between these poles a few more times.

▓ What do you notice?

---

5   Gilbert and Marotos, *Compassionate Mind Training Manual.*

Self-talk and voice tone

How we speak to ourselves internally tells us about the emotional tone of the mind. Think about how you speak to yourself and which voice tone you use – is it neutral, friendly, or harsh and critical? Let's explore that here:

Greet yourself in an unfriendly way, as if you're annoyed at yourself for making a mistake:

Hi (say your name)

Now greet yourself in a friendly tone, as greeting a long-lost friend with as much enthusiasm as you can muster:

Hi (say your name)

Move between the two again. If you wish, you can combine them with hostile/friendly facial expressions.

What do you notice?

What did you notice practising these three exercises?

_____

_____

_____

Why this matters

These exercises are deceptively simple. For example, the regal walking can be done walking around the school building or monitoring students in the classroom. It will help lower the heart rate and for you to feel more grounded and purposeful. The remarkable thing about the facial and self-talk exercises is that they will stimulate mental states. So speaking to yourself in a hostile tone will trigger the fight, flight, freeze response. However, the friendly facial expressions and voice tone will soothe these.

There's an element of 'fake it until you make it' here. Perhaps you have a habit of being harshly critical of yourself. But that's all it is ... a habit. As you have learnt, you can change habits, you can build new neural pathways. By acting *as if* you can be kinder and friendlier to yourself, you will become so. You can adopt different habits and behaviours – ones that in the long run will help you feel happier.

You deserve kindness

Think about this: you are one of nearly eight billion people on this planet. You breathe the same air, you all have the same needs for sustenance, shelter and safety. You all want to connect. Why should you matter any less than anyone else? Why should your needs be less important? It doesn't mean that they are less important, but they certainly aren't more.

This perspective can help because it can strip away feelings of selfishness and guilt. Remember the three systems of emotional regulation discussed in Chapter 3. We all need to learn how to self-soothe, and to continually remind ourselves to do so, because our distress is no less real than anyone else's.

Friendliness meditation

We all do basic things that demonstrate our self-care. We clothe ourselves, brush our teeth, feed ourselves, we don't walk in front of cars. We have a basic interest in keeping ourselves alive and healthy. Just being alive means that we are deserving of kindness and friendliness and by recognising the sanctity of our own life, we can recognise the sanctity of others.

This meditation is in four stages.

Stage one

Establish a comfortable posture, become aware of your body and breath and generally ground yourself. Gradually become aware of your experience and, whatever it is, bring an attitude of kindness, tolerance and acceptance to it. You can do this in many ways – you can focus on pleasurable sensations in the body, like warmth or a relaxed muscle, and allow this to grow. You can repeat phrases to yourself: 'May I be happy, may I be well, may I be free from suffering, may I progress.' You can bring to mind a time when you were really happy. Explore and experiment and find out what works for you.

Stage two

In the second stage, bring to mind a good friend. If you feel kindness for yourself, you will naturally think of those who are nearest and dearest to you. So just as you want to be happy and well, so does your friend and you can wish this for them. You can bring them to mind, perhaps as an image or memory of them when they were really happy and contented. Or you can imagine that they are here with you, breathing in and out just as you are. You can focus on any pleasant physical sensations in your body, like a sense of peace or relaxation, and wish them a similar experience of ease in their own bodies. It's usually better not to bring to mind someone you're sexually attracted to as this confuses the practice, and also not to use a parent/child in this stage as, again, conflicting emotions can arise.

Stage three

So far you've focused on yourself and a good friend. This is relatively easy because you have a strong identification with yourself and likewise a good friend who is in some ways an extension of yourself. The third stage breaks with this convention and asks you to imaginatively connect with someone you've never met, barely noticed and couldn't care less about.

You have plenty of inspiration for the third stage. The 'neutral' person, as they're called, represents the vast sea of humanity: people you know by sight but have no emotional connection with. For example, a member of school staff you don't know, someone who delivers to the school. The neutral person is that person that you see as rather two-dimensional, a cardboard cut-out that forms a backdrop to the drama of your life.

How do you form a connection with someone you barely know? Take them in, what they're wearing, whether they look happy or sad, whether the light is catching their face or it's dulled by cloud. These simple details on a purely physical level can make this person come alive for you.

You can reflect on the fact that just as you are dear to yourself, well so are they dear to themselves. Just as you want to be happy, well so do they. They have their ups and downs, crises and disappointments, just like you. The stories of your lives may differ but the basic human content remains the same. It's about imaginatively identifying with their life, which has a wonderful effect of making you feel more expansive in your life.

It's good to choose the person quickly and not to deliberate and also to stick with the same person for a while. Picture the person in the surroundings you normally see them and wish them to be 'happy, well and free from suffering'.

Stage four

Expand your awareness outwards. Bringing to mind the people in the rest of the house, or that you work with. They all want to be happy and well, so you can wish them so. You can imagine when you breathe out you are breathing a kindly, soothing breath towards them. Gently expand out to neighbours, the community, the wider school community. If it's helpful, repeat to yourself: 'May they be happy, may they be well, may they not be in distress, may they grow and learn.'

Finally, rest back into the feelings of warmth, friendliness and contentment you have created.

What did you notice?

_____

_____

_____

Why does this matter?

Working in a school is an 'other-centred' profession and it's so easy for your needs to get squeezed out. But as referred to in the introduction, if you don't put on the 'oxygen mask' first, then you'll be in no position to help others. Self-care can be counterintuitive and feel selfish. But reflecting on the fact that you are a human being, just like anyone else, means that you have the same needs as others. Unless you can be friendly to yourself, you can't really be friendly to anyone else. There's a solidarity to the friendliness meditation, the fact that every being on this planet wants to be well and doesn't want to suffer. And that includes you. So the question isn't so much, '*Why me?*' but rather, '*Why not me?*'

> You do feel guilty as a head as you naturally want to support others and look after everyone but you need to look after yourself as well. Because if you don't look after yourself and you go down, someone else has got to pick up the pieces and that has a knock-on effect.
>
> (Simon, primary school head teacher)

In this chapter, we've discussed:

- The importance of self-care and nurturing.

- That it's not selfish, it's a crucial part of you being able to do the job you do effectively and care for those in your school community.

- That it might not come easily, but it's something you need to practise so that you can not only survive but thrive. *Neurons that wire together, fire together!*

- That there may be an element of 'fake it until you make it' – by acting in a way that is more friendly towards yourself, even by posture and facial expression, it will become natural.

- That it might still feel like your mind is like 'Teflon for good experiences', but remember what you dwell on grows!

Chapter 9
Mindfulness and Creativity in the Classroom

I knew I had the ability to be a really good teacher, but something was stopping me and I couldn't work out what it was. I realised I was highly tense in the lessons and reacting too quickly in that moment. And the negative self-talk was taking over; I wasn't listening to answers.

(Susan, head of department, secondary school)

What is creativity? We may have a view about whether we are creative or not, or what a creative person looks like, perhaps someone wafting around? However, in an increasingly complex world, we are all being asked to adapt and be flexible to the changing needs of the time. The ability to do this, to think and imagine new ways, is creativity. For example, the difference in educating that COVID-19 has brought about means many school staff have adapted to teaching online, perhaps gaining digital skills and knowledge they had avoided before. Necessity, they say, is the mother of invention. However, whatever your view is of creativity and whether you think you are creative or not, this chapter allows you to explore creativity and how mindfulness can enhance it. Creativity is when we step out of autopilot and habit and do something new. It's a risk, and therefore scary, we don't know how it will go. It's also when we step out of reactivity, and respond to the needs of the moment, opening up to choice. It's a very freeing feeling.

Scientists estimate that around 45% of the choices and decisions we make every day are governed by habit.[1] Nearly half of everything we do! No wonder we feel bored. Why's this? Because having outsourced the routine stuff – such as driving, brushing our teeth – to autopilot, it can start to take over. Habit and autopilot are saying, 'What about this? You don't want to think about that! Let me do that, let me cook that meal or plan that lesson.' Pretty soon, autopilot is running the whole show. We are in cruise control and life feels pretty dull.

---

1 B. Verplanken and W. Wood, Interventions to break and create consumer habits, *Journal of Public Policy and Marketing* 25 (2006): 90–130. Available at: https://journals.sagepub.com/doi/10.1509/jppm.25.1.90.

Habit can get tied up with fear: 'What if something bad happens?' 'Best not to change what works.' This is all very unconscious of course; autopilot is the smooth engine that runs under the bonnet. But being in cruise control can leave us feeling increasingly frustrated, bored or stuck.

Sometimes we want to take the wheel!

So how can mindfulness help? Mindfulness helps us cultivate a new relationship with our experience. Because it involves focus and attention, and being more present, we can become aware of all sorts of thoughts and ideas arising. We can respond to the needs of the moment; for example, if we notice there's a mood of boredom or listlessness in the classroom, we can switch things up and do something else. Research shows that mindfulness helps teachers and lecturers, whatever their subject, to become more reflective teachers, and more skilful and effective in managing their classrooms, delivering impactful teaching and learning, and relating positively to their students.[2]

An example of creativity in the classroom: Supported Learning Experiments

I remember the groans at staff continuing professional development (CPD) days when suddenly we were told we were going to adopt a whole new scheme for literacy or maths. The image of a steamroller came to mind, squashing any progress, learning or valuable evidence from previous systems, and staff in the process! However, when I was teaching, we were also lucky enough to come across the model from colleague and mentor Geoff Petty of Supported Learning Experiments (SLEs).[3]

The idea behind SLEs is that you don't throw the baby out with the bath water (as sometimes advised to do in staff CPD training!). But, for example, out of an hour's lesson, you try something new with the class for 10–15 minutes. You have the security of knowing that you can go back to tried-and-tested ways but have the chance to experiment, innovate and be creative. This could be a new task, a new resource or an interesting new way of introducing a topic. This is a real opportunity for practising mindfulness, to notice the sensations in the body as you step out of your comfort zone, to be alive to

---

2   Hwang et al., A systematic review of mindfulness interventions for in-service teachers.
3   G. Petty, *Evidence-Based Teaching: A Practical Guide* (Cheltenham: Nelson Thomas Ltd, 2006).

the moment, with curiosity. To see how the students respond and feel the excitement or thrill of something new.

When evaluating it, you must be careful not to jump to hasty conclusions. Scientists experiment hundreds of times before reaching a conclusion – you wouldn't want to take medication that had only been tested once. So don't just do it with one class and then assess it, do it with several different classes and reflect. Do it at different times of the day, or at the start, the end or in the middle if energy is flagging. You may decide to tweak, expand or ditch that particular activity and try something else.

It's probably going to feel uncomfortable because it's new. Remember, autopilot has a lot of investment in keeping things the same, keeping the engine ticking over. But be careful not to interpret uncomfortable feelings as data that something is going wrong. It's par for the course when you step outside your comfort zone – remember, *what you can breathe with, you can be with.*

> Coming from being in autopilot in that moment and listening to what the children are saying to you, helps you engage in the lesson so much better. It's changed my life as a teacher and as a parent with my children; it's changed me. Recognising the bodily sensations, where you feel it first and then OK, you can go beyond that, it's uncomfortable but you can go beyond it. The old me wouldn't have noticed that, just would have flicked up the thought, 'OMG I'm a terrible teacher', and I would have just been on the defensive with the children, instead of responding to the moment.
>
> (Susan, head of department, secondary school)

One thing to remember is that if it doesn't go the way you want it to, don't forget your sense of humour. I remember being observed with a class who were resitting their GCSE English. We were engaging with mindful eating, as a way of opening up to the senses and getting the class ready for some creative writing. I asked what a student what he had noticed, and he replied: 'Well it tasted like crap, but I still ate it.'

It was absolutely the last comment I wanted to hear when being observed! But I kept grounded and just reflected back, 'So an unpleasant experience then.'

Creating a mindful setting

Time flies when you are being creative. When you are reactive and in autopilot, time drags. I'm sure you all remember those times when you were absorbed in a task, like cooking or gardening or some sort of craft or painting a fence. Or were lost in a beautiful scene in nature like a sunset. Creativity feels *timeless*.

One of the issues is that you might feel you don't have enough time and space for this to arise. It's hard in busy, working life. However, all the mindfulness exercises in the book so far will help create some space and balance in your life. You'll feel clearer about what you want to do when you have some spare time, rather than the default of being on your phone or watching telly.

In a classroom, you have to set the scene and the conditions for creativity to arise. Lowri is a qualified teacher and works as a TA in an early years setting. She is also a practising artist.

> What they do in school and call 'art' is very formulaic. It's just about the end result and everyone has the same thing. I want to scream because that isn't art. So with drawing, for example, I'd say 'I've got some flowers here'. I would actually have some on the table and I'd say, 'We're really going to look at this flower'. Because otherwise, they will just draw an archetype of a flower rather than really looking at it. I've been trying to bring mindfulness into that so that they are observing what they're draw- ing. Looking at the colour and saying, 'Oh, look at that yellow. Maybe we need to make it a bit lighter – so how are we going to do that?' I was getting them to paint with the breath, with each stroke. Some of those boisterous boys, you wouldn't think they would do it but they actually love it. That's a skill that you can teach.

This mindful approach hasn't just improved their creative skills; it's improved their focus and attention too.

> Before, they'd all be chatting and not really paying attention to what they were doing. Slowing down and almost bringing a meditative process, it's quite incredible the results you get. In terms of the quality of their drawing, it's a 100% better – as they're tapping into their own inner world instead of being busy and then just drawing and scribbling.

What Lowri is describing is really important, because she is providing a way for young children to access their inner world and resources, their imagination. She's giving them the physical skills too, but using mindfulness to cultivate the imaginative faculty means that in time they'll have the ability and confidence to choose materials to draw or rep- resent something and each piece of work will be unique.

Having the confidence to experiment and try new things is a powerful exemplification to your students. It communicates that they can take a risk with answers, try to see something from another angle, rather than getting defeated and giving up.

Convergent and divergent thinking

Convergent thinking is another term for problem-solving. It's the idea that there's an answer, somewhere out there, a tried-and-tested solution. It relies on rationality, logic and experience. It's an important and pragmatic skill. However, the danger with over-reliance on convergent thinking is that it is a gateway for habit and autopilot. We do what we have always done and hope for the best. Or there is an issue to be solved, perhaps an uncomfortable one. It can be characteristic of the threat zone we explored in Chapter 3. Instead of turning towards the uncomfortable feelings/thoughts that it stimulates and giving them some space, we want to get rid of the problem. We want to go for a quick fix. The trouble with this approach is that it may have solved the issue in the short to medium term, but it's ignored other possibilities yet unexplored, which may lead to a more satisfying and sustainable solution.

Dr Danny Penman calls divergent thinking 'true creativity'.[4] The gratification of a quick solution is deferred while many different options are explored, sometimes in parallel. Dreaming, musing, exploring different possibilities with no fixed agenda are all involved in divergent thinking. In short, being present to our experience, how it is and giving it space is divergent thinking. Being curious about possibilities is divergent thinking; being able to listen to the ideas of others, perhaps even critical voices, is divergent thinking. It's most prevalent in people who are non-conformist, willing to take risks, are resilient with setbacks – an example of this is Steve Jobs. Some education leaders have found that mindfulness has given them permission to take their time over big decisions and see the value of it. Sam is the CEO of a large FE college:

> I like to look at the issue from different angles. I pose the question to my staff, 'That one person who is resisting or disagrees with this proposal, what if they're right?'

Where convergent thinking is associated with the threat circle, divergent thinking is associated with the soothing mode circle of the system of regulation. Funnily enough, many people associate this circle with being passive, being a dreamer and doing nothing. But in fact, when you're in that circle, you feel safe and secure. This opens up the possibility of being brave, taking risks and not getting deflated when you meet the setbacks that life inevitably holds. The difficult time of the pandemic and the crisis it has brought to schools and colleges has brought about the opportunity to do things radically differently. Sandra has found it has brought about much more awareness on the importance of team relationships in the department she runs:

---

4   Penman, *Mindfulness for Creativity*, p. 17.

We've had a rota where less staff are physically in and it means you have more quality interactions. I've invited someone to have a walking meeting or discuss things on a park bench. Definitely, I want to hold on to some of these things when things go back after COVID.

(Sandra, head of ALN, FE college)

You can see how mindfulness underpins convergent and divergent thinking. By stepping out of autopilot and being open and present to our experience, however it is, with kindness and curiosity, brings about its own fruits. You can enjoy this process of giving space, the excitement of seeing what emerges and feel free to explore and play with ideas.

Mindfulness exercises to try

Habit releasers

Stepping out of autopilot takes effort, but you can start with the little things. There are suggestions below of small things you could do differently each day and notice the effect. You could adopt one and follow it through the week or perhaps do one for half a week and then another for the other half. The main thing is to be curious and playful about this, rather than rigid and fixed. Don't let the habit releaser become another habit!

Suggestions of what you could do are:

- Eat something different for breakfast each day.

- Take a different route to your school/college.

- Sit in a different chair in the staff room.

- Wear something you keep 'for best' to work.

- Try out an SLE – improvise for 15 minutes of a lesson.

- Nominate different people to answer questions.

- Go out for a cuppa with a colleague at lunchtime.

- Choose a different walking/running route.

- Let your dog take you for a walk! Follow their lead.

- Try cooking something new.

- Eat or get takeout from a restaurant you've always fancied.

- Contact an old friend.

- Go vegan for a day.

- Go on an artist's date – put in your diary that exhibition, film or theatre production you've wanted to see and treat it like a doctor or dentist appointment (something you can't miss).

- Enrol for something you've never done before – a salsa class, water-colour painting, kick-boxing.

You probably have your own ideas, in which case, feel free to follow them! The possibilities are literally endless and do not need to be 'useful' in any way.

What did you notice?

	What did you do?	How was that?
Monday		
Tuesday		
Wednesday		
Thursday		
Friday		
Saturday		
Sunday		

Why does this matter?

Habits are how autopilot manifests in our life, so even making small changes can have an effect and shake things up, changing our perspective. By starting with changing little things and being curious about the effect, you can gain confidence and learn to trust your inner wisdom and intuition a bit more. The effect of this can be powerful; you feel more alive and life seems fresher and more vibrant.

The nine dots exercise

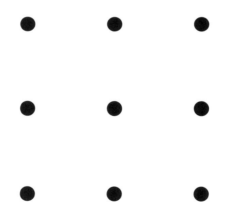

Without lifting your pen from the paper, connect these nine dots by using four straight lines.

What do you notice?

- Determination before you start, you need to get this right! How does this show up in the body? A gritted jaw, for example.

- Fear: 'I'll look stupid if I don't get this right!' How does this show up in the body? Your heart might start racing, for example.

- Frustration: 'Why can't I do this?' How does this show up? Tightness or tension.

- Giving up: 'What's the point?' Perhaps this manifests itself through a slumped posture.

The answer

The key to the nine dots exercise is having a broader perspective than what's in front of you. If we extend the lines outside the dots, then it can be done. The problem is that we see the problem as the nine dots itself, rather than the area and space around it. By stepping back, and giving space, the answer can become clear. The four suggestions of what you might have noticed when doing this exercise, show up habitual ways that you react to a problem or difficulty. Autopilot blocks creativity, so you need to see outside the frame.

Wobbling and staying still[5]

Stand and take a few breaths. Keep your eyes open.

Raise one foot off the floor. It doesn't need to be particularly high, just so that you're slightly unbalanced. If balance is an issue for you, you can do this sitting down and shift your weight to the edge of the seat so that you have minimal support, then raise one knee up.

Now try and stay still. Do your best to stay still and not to wobble.

---

5   S. Silverton, *Living in the Present: Teaching Notes* (Conwy: The Present CIC, 2020).

What happens?

_____

_____

_____

_____

_____

Now actively invite wobble: raise your foot in the air, an arm in another direction. Do an aeroplane position like you might have done as child in the playground, anything that creates wobble.

Do not try and stay still – wobble as much as you can!

What happens?

_____

_____

_____

_____

_____

What did you notice?

_____

_____

_____

Why this matters

When doing this exercise, most people find that when they are unbalanced and trying to impose stillness, they can't stop wobbling and may fall over. However, when they invite wobbling, something in them knows how to keep them balanced and stops them from falling over.

Those of us of a certain age will remember the Weebles toys ('Weebles wobble, but they don't fall down!'). It's the same with your minds and bodies: you are more resilient than you think. If you have a harsh view of yourself, think you should be coping better than you are or be different, that makes you feel wobbly, frightened, insecure. However, if you allow yourself to wobble, knowing that this is an inevitable part of living, of being a human being, then strength comes from the most unexpected places. You find you can stand strong like a tree, even if you're being buffeted by the wind.

The Goose and the Bottle

There is a goose inside the bottle.
There is a bottle with a goose inside.
How does the goose get out of the bottle?
How does it stay alive?
How does the bottle stay unbroken?
Where is the goose? Where is the bottle?
You are the goose. You are the bottle.
You are the goose inside the bottle.
Close your eyes: the goose is inside the bottle.
Say it: the goose is out of the bottle.
Believe it: the bottle is not broken, the goose alive.

Open your eyes: the goose is out of the bottle.
There is the goose. There is the bottle.
You have become the goose out of the bottle.
You are not broken. You are alive.

Linda France[6]

This poem is a puzzle – and, like the nine dots, at first it seems impossible to solve. How can a goose be in a bottle? How can it stay alive? You can try to think your way through it in a convergent way, battle it with will, get frustrated, but it doesn't work. That's because it cannot be solved on that level. Rather you need to let go, take a step back and see afresh. Then, magically, the goose is out of the bottle but both goose and bottle are intact. By engaging in this divergent thinking, something unexpected can arise. It's not about problem-solving or fixing life, as often life can be mysterious. As the poem says: 'You are not broken. You are alive.'

In this chapter, we've learnt:

- Mindfulness can enhance the creativity and therefore quality of your teaching.

- By being present, you are more alive to the students and can harness their energy and flow.

- Creativity is a risk – stepping out of autopilot can be scary and may feel uncomfortable.

- You can start small, trying different things, and try not get deflated if they don't go the way you want them to.

- The difference between convergent and divergent thinking, how we need both but to be aware of convergent thinking taking over all the time.

- You need to be willing to step back, let go, see the space around the activity.

- Importantly, you are exemplifying qualities of creativity to the students, who will have to navigate an increasingly complex world and will need to have skills of thinking 'outside the box'.

---

6   L. France, *The Heart as Origami* (London: Parallax Press, 2005).

Chapter 10

Under Pressure

From Surviving to Thriving

Whether you've got a project or a deadline, a pile of marking or a report to compile, working in a school/college means you've constantly got a 'to do' list. There are pressures and pinch points to the year, which means at times you will be working under conditions of sustained stress. So how can you manage this and not only survive under these conditions but thrive?

> There's things on your desk: budget, fire safety issues, HR issues, staffing issues, parent issues. You end up doing a little bit of this and a little bit of that and you just don't end up getting anything done.
>
> (Ewan, primary school head teacher)

The Yerkes–Dodson Law (1908) shows that a little bit of stress is good for you. It can motivate you and get you out of bed in the morning.[1] You put energy and effort into something and you see the results. The difficulty is when the level of stress rises to a point where you feel you can't manage it; you are drowning in tasks and feel overwhelmed. Motivation gets replaced with despondency, focus is replaced with confusion. At this point, you've passed the peak of performance and are heading for fatigue and even breakdown and burnout. So how can mindfulness help?

When first learning about mindfulness, there's a lot of focus on the body. This is because the body acts as a barometer and can give you early indications of what's going on.

Remember waiting to go into an exam hall and having sweating palms or feeling as if you had butterflies in your stomach? Feeling like you might throw up or suddenly needing to go to the toilet? These bodily sensations indicate the hallmarks of stress and our fight, flight and freeze system kicking in. What happens, quite quickly, is that you register them as being pleasant, painful or plain. And from there you start either to want to

---

1 M. Chaskalson, *The Mindful Workplace: Developing Resilient Individuals and Resonant Organisations with MBSR* (Chichester: Wiley-Blackwell, 2011).

pull it towards you, like an ice cream (yum!) or push it away, like an exam (yuck!) – or in the case of plain, you just don't really register it or feel a bit blank.

So this is why it's really important to learn to notice what sensations are happening in the body:

- Tightness?

- Heat?

- Tingling?

- Fizzing?

and how you are *relating* to them: do they induce

- Pleasant, painful or plain feelings?

Exercise: Exploring feelings of stress in the body and stressful thoughts in the mind

The first step to thriving rather than surviving is to become aware of how stress manifests in our body and mind. Here is a scenario exercise to help you discern what kind of bodily sensations, emotions and thoughts occur when we are triggered by stress.

Sit comfortably and close your eyes if that feels OK, or if not then keep your gaze soft and unfocused and visualise the following scene in your mind's eye:

It's Friday afternoon and you're just finishing some last jobs at your desk before the weekend. A school staff member walks in and drops a load of books on your desk. Someone is off sick from today and these books need to be moderated over the weekend to meet a deadline.

▦ First, what happens in the body when you visualise this/read these words? Any tension or tightening? Where?

▦ Second, what's your interpretation of these bodily sensations? Pleasant? Painful? Plain?

▦ Third, what emotions or thoughts come up? Surprise? Fear? Anxiety? Thoughts such as 'This isn't fair!', 'That messes up my weekend plans.'

▦ Finally, what actions or impulses immediately arise? Wanting to shove the books back at them? Or storm down the corridor to see the head teacher?

Note your responses here:

Bodily sensations	Interpretation of these sensations: pleasant, painful or plain?	Thoughts or emotions in the moment	Immediate actions or impulses

Why does this matter?

Think back to the stress cycle in Chapter 5. By starting to pay attention to these bodily sensations, *the sweating palms*, *the knot in the stomach*, you can recognise what is happening. It'll be fairly clear whether it feels pleasant, painful or plain. But watch what happens next – the whirlwind of thoughts, the actions and impulses being activated in your system. You may feel yourself lurch forward, or withdraw back involuntarily. This all happens so quickly – in a heartbeat, in a mind moment. This is when we need to pay attention and create a gap.

Creating a gap means creating some space between your thoughts/emotions and your actions. Between your internal world and your external world. You can do this by using the practices you've already been learning to soothe the nervous system, such as the emotional barometer, the mindful minute or the three-step breathing space. This is what it means to *respond* rather than *react*.

The first step is to recognise what is happening: that you are working on parallel tasks, and the pressure is mounting.

> I realised that my role was constantly pushing me into forward thinking. I was always thinking 'What do I do now? What do I do next?' It's good to sit back and think 'How have things gone? What could we do differently? What's a priority at the moment?' Rather than get in the flow of the next thing and the next thing.
>
> (Sandra, head of ALN, FE college)

Mindfulness exercises to try

From scattered to focused

Spend a few moments tuning in to yourself, either sitting down or using mindful movement.

What's the emotional weather?

Where can you feel this pressure or distraction in the body?

- Tension somewhere in the body – such as in the neck or shoulders, or stomach possibly?

- A feeling of restlessness and fidgeting?

- General sense of feeling all over the place, swaying, off balance?

- Tiredness and heaviness?

Whatever you experience, accept and allow it. This is how it feels now, but it's not fixed – it can also change.

Take a few deeper and more intentional breaths.

Broaden out your awareness to the whole of you sitting here – your physicality, what you can hear around you, the breath flowing in and out. In this way, you can have the sense of being a bigger container where things rise and fall, moment by moment. You can sit in flow, noticing what is arising without getting caught up in it.

Remember to have that kind, curious attitude. You are doing your best.

Engage with the day again.

What did you notice?

_____

_____

_____

_____

_____

Why this matters

What you're doing is acknowledging how things are in this moment and giving it some space. Remember, you're not trying to fix anything here; you're not even trying to change anything. Trying involves tension. You are softening any extra tension that you might be bringing to the situation by thinking it should or shouldn't be happening. You are responding, not reacting.

Nobody likes being stressed or what it brings up in them. Sometimes your bodies and minds can feel like a wild animal, caged up. The tendency is to either try and fix it, causing the animal to rail against the bars even more, or just try and ignore it and push it away, making the animal whimper or growl. Neither work. But by creating a gap, you give that difficulty some space, and give yourself some room to breathe. The fear might be that if you acknowledge what is happening, you might go out of control. But if you give the animal more space, it might buck and bound around to start with, but eventually it will run itself out and settle down. This is what it means to become a bigger container, to hold your experience.

Not surviving but thriving

You want to get past that feeling of just getting through the day that is governed by fight, flight and freeze. Instead you want to feel like you are enjoying parts of your life, that you become alive and feel energised by them. The first step is look at how you're spending your time.

> I know what nourishes me and I know what depletes me, but sometimes I choose not to nourish myself and I'll fall into a rut. However, I'll soon notice this neglect and then I'll get back on it, without beating myself up about it. Then I'll make time to have those moments of self-care. I'll run without music, I want to feel alive.
>
> (Simon, primary school head teacher)

Nourishing/depleting activities

Spend a few minutes thinking of the broad set of activities that make up your working day from the moment you get up to going to bed. Write them down in a list with a space next to them, for example:

Wake up

Cup of tea

Shower

Make packed lunches

When it comes to work, instead of just writing 'work', be specific – such as 'morning meeting', 'teaching', 'yard duty'. Although, equally, don't feel like you have to give a blow-by-blow account; broad brushstrokes will do. I had a deputy head once who had filled a side of A4 and only got to 'morning break'!

Once you've completed the list, go through them again and put an 'N' next to them if you find them nourishing. A 'D' next to them if you find them depleting and a '−' next to them if they are neither/nor. Don't overthink this, just go with what your gut is telling you as you move down the list.

What did you notice?

When you have done this, take a moment and scan the list. Does anything stand out for you? On one occasion that I completed this exercise, I realised how stressful I found the school run, everyone getting ready to go out on time with the inevitable scramble for coats and shoes. I reflected: could I put a mindful moment in there so it didn't feel so pressurised? Or there might be something that you thought you didn't enjoy but actually you put an N next to it. Take a moment to reflect.

Why this matters

Going back to the exhaustion funnel in Chapter 4, does the list reflect you keeping a broad range of activities in your life? If something is nourishing, could you do more of it? Or if something is depleting, could you do a bit less of it? When I did this exercise, I realised how much I was checking my work email from home in the evening and weekends and resolved not to do this unless there was a very good reason. We all have tasks in our lives that we don't want to but have to do – this is a big part of being an adult. But you can still exercise awareness and conscious choice around this. Can you approach rather than avoid the activity?

> I've learnt not to overstretch myself beyond what I think I can do, so I know that I've got to know myself better. I need to be mindful of my tendency to overwork or become obsessive or to overpromise. I'm also prone to agreeing to things and becoming a bit manic when feeling good and then thinking, 'I shouldn't have done

that'. But now I feel more aware of when to say no and of my own limitations – and I have more clarity and assertiveness around letting people know that.

(Sian, Healthy Schools co-ordinator, secondary school)

Have a look at the instances of '–' on your list. Are these activities that you might find nourishing sometimes and depleting at other times? Why is this? Take a moment to reflect. Often it can be factors like tiredness or our mood that can affect how you perceive something. When you are tired or stressed, you will naturally fall into autopilot, doing what you've always done and hoping for the best. What would it take for you to adjust your attitude, so that something you're resisting feels manageable?

Often we think we need to make big changes in our life for it feel different, but just small tweaks can make a difference. Doing the breathing space with action step and asking yourself, 'How can I best take care of myself now?' can open up possibilities. You might decide to switch off the television or the computer in the evening and do something you find a bit more nourishing, such as reading or having a bath. It's not that there's anything wrong with watching the television or spending time online, it's more about making a conscious choice about what nourishes you and how to spend your time.

A special educational needs teacher who attended one of my courses commented that she loved watching historical documentaries. But she had got into the habit of googling facts while she was watching them, so ended up missing half the documentary and felt wired, not relaxed, at the end. You are getting to know your own mind and your own tendencies. By first recognising these, without harsh self-criticism, you can bring awareness to them. Then you can make a choice: 'Do I want to carry on like this? Or can I try something different?'

Use this table to help you reflect:

Which activities do you find nourishing and you can find a bit more time for?
1 For example: exercise
2
3
4
5
Which activities do you find depleting and you need to do a bit less of?
1 For example: checking email outside work hours
2
3
4
5
Which activities are either nourishing or depleting depending on mood? What could you adjust to make them more pleasant?
1 For example: on yard duty, I could notice my surroundings and body as I walk around the school
2
3
4
5

I found mindfulness works day to day, and not just in work. I like sports, such as surfing and cycling, and I've found that rather than striving, I'm being present and going for it. It's helped my performance tenfold, in both cycling and surfing, and in anything else that I do. It all comes together: if your home life is more relaxed, your school life is more relaxed. It helps your sleep, too.

(Josh, secondary school teacher)

The value of practising mindfulness is that your awareness will grow. You will get to know yourself better and therefore your strengths and limitations, which we all have. By becoming clearer and developing the ability to step back that mindfulness practice gives you, you can make wise choices about what you do or don't do. I remember getting myself into states at work, feeling overwhelmed but thinking, '*Yes but I've got to*'. When you get into that mindset, you've lost sight of the fact that you have a choice. Sure, there are things you *have* to do at work, but how, and in what manner you do them, is up to you. And you do have a choice about extra things that you take on. Sometimes when I am weighing this up, I think of my life without the extra thing. If I feel a sense of relief, I know it's not the right thing for me. Stepping back opens up choice and initiative, and what comes with this is a sense of confidence and empowerment.

In this chapter, we've discussed that:

■ A little bit of stress is good for you but too much means you get overwhelmed and are surviving.

- The first step is to notice the signature of stress through bodily sensations, thoughts and feelings, and then act accordingly.

- It is easy when stressed to become scattered and inefficient. Bringing awareness to this can help us recollect our purpose and feel like we have the initiative.

- We thrive when we respond, rather than react. This means taking stock and doing something in the moment that takes account our whole being.

- By reflecting on what you find nourishing, depleting and neutral, you bring more choice into how to manage your day.

You won't always manage it, but by having the intention of thriving rather than surviving, you'll manage it more often than not. As Mike, a primary school teacher, says:

> The next moment is the next moment, it's what you do now that matters. If it's gone, and you've had a stressful morning, take that breath and move on. This is now. Those are the challenges, those days where you think, I meant to take a breath, I meant to have that moment and I didn't because I forgot. It's really hard sometimes but you've just got to be kind to yourself. Tomorrow's another day.

Chapter 11
Becoming a Mindfulness Champion

Good teachers are at the heart of any effective classroom, and any good school, and mindful teachers are at the heart of mindfulness in schools.[1]

You may have been enjoying reading this book, using the practices and thinking it can benefit others in your school/college. Perhaps you're fired up by some of the ideas and would like to share these with the learners. In the majority of cases, mindfulness in schools/colleges is grown by people like you: champions – who, having had some experience and practice of mindfulness, can see the benefits and potential and want to pass it on to others. You are the members of staff who will be willing to give up a lunchtime or run an after-school club to share your enthusiasm.

What does being a mindfulness champion in a school/college community mean? How can you gain the confidence and competence to pass the skills on to others? How can you convince 'the powers that be' that this is what the school/college really needs?

What does it mean to be a mindfulness champion?

First of all, being a mindfulness champion is about having a regular mindfulness practice yourself. That doesn't mean meditating for an hour every day, but it does mean that you make time for regular practice and try to keep a flow of mindfulness going throughout your day. You might value feeling steady, calm and grounded, and can notice when you aren't these things and know how to bring yourself back to these states. You may do this by engaging in short practices, punctuated throughout the day, such as the breathing space, the mindful minute, or mindful walking around the school or college. It also might be that you regularly engage in longer practices you've learnt in this book, like the playful body scan, breath and body meditation or mindful movement. It's challenging to find regular time in an already busy schedule to practice. So creating a mindset and making it part of your daily routine is key.

---

1   Weare and Bethune, *Implementing Mindfulness in Schools*, p. 53.

I realised that you could take certain aspects of it and make it work for you, rather than feeling like you had to shoehorn it in. I enjoy mindfulness when I'm physically moving, like walking. I notice the colours in the sky, the wisps of cloud and how beautiful it is. It lifts me.

(Claire, well-being and safeguarding manager, FE college)

Ashridge Business School undertook some research with busy managers engaging in a mindfulness programme.[2] They found out that those who engaged with at least 10 minutes of mindfulness practice every day reported improvements in resilience, collaboration, agility, perspective taking, empathy, as well as sleep and stress levels. This could be longer practices such as meditation, body scan or mindful movement, or a number of shorter practices such as the three-step breathing space, mindful minute and so on. And if you want to do more than 10 minutes a day – that's great!

Why does this matter?

Mindfulness is *caught* not *taught,* and having your own practice means that you are embodying these values or calmness, perspective and positive engagement. This alone will make an impression on staff and students around you: they'll notice that you remain calm in stressful times, don't get so blown about by things and maintain a perspective. It will influence others without you having to speak directly about mindfulness. Equally, if you don't practise what you preach, others will pick up on it.

---

2   M. Chaskalson and M. Reitz, *Mind Time: How 10 Mindful Minutes Can Enhance Your Work, Health and Happiness* (London: Thorsons, 2018).

How can you gain the confidence and competence to pass the skills on to others?

I have interacted with hundreds of school and college champions, trying to bring mindfulness into their own establishment, as well as having my own journey with this. I would like to share some of their stories with you.

The following case studies derive from Wales where exciting things are happening in mindfulness. The context for this is having the Centre for Mindfulness Research and Practice at Bangor University for the last 20 years. But also the development of the new schools curriculum for Wales, due to be implemented in 2022, which has been co-produced with members of the profession.[3] This curriculum sets out to encourage ambitious, capable learners, ready to learn throughout life. It has six areas of learning and experience, including one on health and well-being, where mental health is as prominent as physical health. Each area has a 'What matters' subheading and educators have grasped the relevance and adaptability of mindfulness to grow these core skills and competences under these headings. Therefore, there has been an appetite to try out mindfulness and embrace the benefits, leading to a number of examples of best practice. Here are three examples from early years, primary and secondary schools.

Early years setting

Teacher A was an additional learning needs coordinator (ALN-CO) who introduced mindfulness to the independent school where she worked. She arranged a Mindful Well-being day for the school sixth form, run by properly trained mindfulness instructors. The day was a huge success and students asked for further mindfulness sessions. Based on the feedback, the ALN-CO was able to have a .b course (Mindfulness in Secondary Schools[4]) commissioned in 2019. While the original participants became too busy to engage with the course, students from Years 8 and 9 participated in the 10-week programme along with the ALN-CO. In total, 100% said they found the course enjoyable and 80% said they would continue practising in some form, citing better sleeping and eating habits as a result of the course.

---

3   For more information, see https://hwb.gov.wales/curriculum-for-wales.
4   The Mindfulness in Schools Project – see Resources.

Inspired by the .b course, the teacher engaged in her own mindfulness training, participating in an eight-week MBCT for stress course to further her knowledge and experience: 'Immediately I felt calmer and was noticing more. Before I'd been living on autopilot.'

By growing her awareness, she realised that her heart was no longer in being an ALN-CO. An opportunity arose that year for her to return to early years teaching in the school setting and, in 2019, she trained in 'The Present', a mindfulness spiral curriculum for 3–14 years (see Resources). The Present training encourages attention and noticing, being very aware of things around and changes, and taking time to notice that being woven through the day.

She taught 44 early years children per year group.

> Thinking about teaching younger children early on in my career, we'd talk about all the changes in spring time and so on, but we wouldn't actually give much time for the children to experience it. It was something I had to do, to get done.

Mindfulness has given her confidence in her teaching method:

> Now I think, 'I don't care how long it takes, we will stop and look at things and take notice of what the children have found, regardless of what lesson we're supposed to be doing'. I think that's really important for the younger ones.

She comments that without that it's really difficult for the younger children to focus and build the quality of attention that they're capable of. She acknowledges that working in earlier years makes it easier, as the day can be more fluid, rather than the need to cram lots of things in. An example of this was on St David's Day. The children sat looking at daffodils outside, then they closed their eyes and felt the sun of their faces. As they did this, they imagined being like a daffodil, opening and reaching up to the sun. Afterwards, they drew daffodils, and there was lots of lovely engagement and positive conversation.

She ran a mindfulness after-school club too, but it was interesting that after the second week some parents thought that they had signed their children up to a 'colouring club'. The perception was of mindfulness being an activity rather than something to be experienced and cultivated. Overall, the club and the feedback from parents was positive, but she has found that the engagement with mindfulness and benefits are readily seen when it's woven throughout the day.

Mindful activities were shared for all primary children during the pandemic as part of remote learning. The experience led naturally to lots more time to experience and reflect on the natural world around them and look at it more closely – discussing the changes they observed day by day and how these changes effected their emotions and behaviour.

On returning to school, the staff found themselves reflecting upon the experience in their current practice – planning to provide greater opportunities for noticing and reflection. The Curriculum for Wales has a greater focus on this too, with planning in the moment given greater weight than before. From staff there is acknowledgment of positive learning throughout the pandemic with the benefits of being more mindful in their day-to-day lives than ever before.

One of the main barriers to a whole-school approach to mindfulness is that staff see mindfulness as just another thing to do, more work for them. So some work needs to be done to talk about the benefits of practising mindfulness in terms of work/life balance.

> Mindfulness can be so simple. If you didn't know, you wouldn't think you were practising it. And if you don't know about it then you can't value it.

Primary school

Teacher B attended a mindfulness taster session, and on the basis of that engaged with an eight-week mindfulness course run by his teaching union. 'I thought teaching is a stressful job and this is going to be helpful so that's what drew me in.' On the course his instructor said that if he carried on his mindfulness practice, he could train to teach it to the children in his primary school class. 'That was a big motivator for me. I didn't even know that mindfulness in schools was a thing.'

In 2016, he trained in Paws b, the Mindfulness in Schools Project's mindfulness programme for primary school (see Resources). He started teaching it to his class and was pleased when pupils started to use the language and the science of mindfulness to discuss their states of mind. 'My amygdala was too quick for me!' one boy said after an incident the playground. The school had also engaged in restorative approaches training for a positive school ethos, and the teacher found that mindfulness blended well with the reflective nature of the practice.

At the end of the course, the teacher offered a drop-in Mindfulness Club one lunchtime a week. The children were welcome to come along and practise together and to talk about how they use mindfulness outside lessons. He also trained in 'The Present'. The club had a number of regular members but they tended to be the enthusiastic ones rather than attracting a wide group. He decided to survey children that he had taught Paws b to in previous years by creating a brief online questionnaire, asking the children from his previous classes to respond. The response was heartening. In total, 95% said that they had enjoyed doing the Paws b course when they were in his class. They remembered most of the practices, and he was delighted to discover that two-thirds of them still used them at least sometimes. Five children revealed that they practised daily. Most revealing of all, perhaps, was the fact that only half the children surveyed knew about the Mindfulness Club – and 27 of them said they would like to come! Carrying out the survey renewed his confidence that teaching mindfulness is of benefit to children and left him feeling inspired to 'grow' mindfulness further at his school. He has since relaunched the school mindfulness club. He currently works as a permanent cover teacher and so is able to share some mindfulness in all classes that he teaches.

In 2017 he engaged in school mindfulness lead training, allowing him to teach adult mindfulness courses to colleagues in his school and the school cluster he belonged to. He has also trained in 'Living in the Present', the adult version of 'The Present' course. However, the opportunities to train colleagues in school time have been scarce:

> It's been a slow process, a drip-drip effect. Some teachers did the initial mindfulness course, but that was for their own well-being. One teacher in early years has done The Present training too so that makes a difference. Hopefully with the new curriculum there will be the time and space to give these children the experience.

Secondary faith school

Teacher C teaches in a Catholic high school in South Wales that serves 11–16-year-olds within the area. She had already attended a mindfulness course for her own well-being: she was on anti-depressants after suffering from post-natal depression and didn't want that to be the long-term solution. She recognised she needed a way to manage stressful thoughts in her mind. The mindfulness course helped her to unpick incidents and behaviours and find some perspective:

> You know that you have an inner calm – no matter what problem gets thrown at you. The issue with school is that lack of autonomy in the day, where kids pull your attention, teachers pull your attention, and there's the expectation that you go with it, that they're allowed to do that and hijack your attention. For me, mindfulness has set that inner calm and intention, and I feel that I can direct it towards something when I feel like I'm ready, when I can cope with it.

As well as helping her own mental health, she was aware that mental health statistics gathered within her school suggested that an increasing number of pupils were accessing or needing the help of the school counsellor. She attended 'Mindfulness Champions Training', a short course run by Breathworks (see Resources), which is designed to help those enthusiastic about mindfulness to share their practice. The course focuses on giving participants the confidence and competence to lead meditation. She enjoyed the course, and after completing it, she ran a voluntary lunchtime club for pupils. She discovered that the benefits of this were:

- 100% pupils agreed they had learnt a new skill that helped them with their home life and, when discussed further, some commented on how it quietened the mind during prayer time in school and at home.

- Pupils had somewhere to go. They had chosen to come, and it was a positive way to generate pupil interest and successful for a pastoral intervention.

- There was positive feedback from both parents, pupils and other stakeholders.

However, being a faith school, there was some concern that this was in conflict with the faith or 'Buddhism by the back door'. To answer this concern with rigour, she decided to engage in a professional enquiry. She applied to the Local Education Consortium (a super local authority) and was successful in obtaining some funding to investigate, 'Can mindfulness complement the practice of Christian meditation in a school to support the development of health and well-being?' As part of this enquiry, she was able to train in Mindfulness for Schools Project's .b – a programme for secondary school children consisting of 10 lessons with the option of 4 top-up lessons (see Resources). The next step was to teach this curriculum to 32 Year 7 pupils. This was part of a 'conscript' group – that is, it happened during timetabled lessons. The teacher was successful in obtaining this time by teachers 'gifting' lessons. The results were promising:

- It was viewed as an important part of the curriculum, which ties in with the findings about pupil views in the School Health Research Network's School Environment questionnaire.

- A pupil commented, 'When I am upset, it helps calm me down. Sometimes I focus on my breathing ... it helps me concentrate while working.'

- A parent commented, 'My daughter managed to sleep after her doing her well-being exercise before bed. She has always had a problem sleeping at night.'

- 75% of those who took part said they would recommend it to a friend.

The disadvantages were:

- A conscript class meant pupils missed lessons they might not have wanted to.

- There is only one teacher trained to teach mindfulness at the moment.

There was a proposal to teach mindfulness to pupils in transition from primary to secondary school. Transition, and how it is managed, is key to the happiness and well-being of a young learner. Empowering a pre-teen with knowledge of how their mind works would be invaluable before the storm of adolescence starts to erupt. The research evidence indicates that real positive change can happen when transition programmes are well-designed and effective. The feeder primary schools were interested, but due to the COVID-19 pandemic, engagement was difficult. Also, aspects of well-being were being taught through a broader well-being intervention.

Teacher C is now developing a well-being project as part of physical education lessons and being used to address groups of pupils who are not currently taking part for a range of issues. Sessions addressing body image, the mind and well-being are being taught weekly through mindful movement with pupils.

In answer to the teacher's professional enquiry about whether mindfulness can complement Christian meditation in school to develop health and well-being, she found the crossovers are evident with the opportunity to sit in silence and contemplate. Mindfulness can bring focus and a sense of presence to these moments, rather than being distracted with thoughts of future/past, making this a valuable pause for teachers and students in the school day. All students in feeder primary schools engage with a daily examen prayer and in secondary school a weekly prayer led by the chaplain over the public address system. However, there are multiple opportunities for meaningful silence within the school day, and both mindfulness and prayer improve well-being through a sense of belonging.

Why this matters

Confidence and competence are key to successful delivery. It's a big step to go from practising for yourself to sharing/guiding others. So give yourself the resources and time it needs – make sure whatever training programme you're involved in gives you opportunities to practise sharing with others and gain feedback. It's much better to guide practices first with peer learners, rather than go 'live' for the first time with senior managers or learners who might be cynical about the whole thing. Avoid using recordings if you can – it's far more authentic coming from you. Money is usually tight, and if budget holders have the idea that they can get away with playing YouTube clips instead of investing in proper training, they probably will.

Mindfulness champions: takeaways

▪ Be clear about your next steps. For you that might be engaging with more training to confidently share mindfulness practices with staff or learners. There are examples of credible programmes by properly qualified teachers and trainers in the Resources section.

Please note that you don't need to train to be an adult mindfulness teacher. This is a lengthy and costly route, and there are many training programmes more suitable for workplace and education training.

Start small: with staff, this might include sharing a five-minute practice, in a staff briefing, team meeting with some colleagues. Most staff really enjoy the space and quiet and opportunity to take a moment; this is what usually sells it to them. With learners, there are specific curricula you can train in or you may want to experiment with weaving some practices through the day. There are some ideas how to do this with all ages in the next chapter. It also might be worth offering a short mindfulness taster to parents too so that they can understand what mindfulness is about.

▪ Be flexible and opportunistic. Even if your school does invest in your training, releasing you or others off timetable to teach mindfulness lessons is another story. Take what opportunities are there, well-being days, inset days. I started by teaching two mindfulness lessons together, every fortnight. This wasn't ideal, but it got my foot in the door. Staff saw how children were in the lessons and the effect the practices had on them. This will convince staff, particularly sceptical ones, of the value of what you are trying to do.

▪ Create opportunities – start a lunchtime or afternoon club for the learners. This might not be your ideal scenario, but you will start to build a small cohort of school champions, and word of mouth in a school community is the most powerful driver. One mindfulness trainer colleague told me that her school club immediately became popular when the school rugby star started attending. He was interested in hearing about how Jonny Wilkinson used mindfulness to focus to kick his penalties and the crossovers with sports psychology.

▪ Once the learners are established in their practices, have a school assembly or presentation that includes them. Give them the opportunity to talk about how mindfulness has helped them and, if possible, get them to lead a short practice. Everyone who works in a school/college is usually committed to their learners' well-being. It's extraordinarily powerful hearing learners speak about how they've been able to manage difficulty and thrive. I promise you, there won't be a dry eye in the house.

How can you convince senior leadership that this is what the school/college really needs?

Even if an organisation invests in your training, it can still be a challenge to gain the full mandate to teach. So find an ally in senior leadership or on the governors' board – someone who appreciates these values and has the well-being of staff and learners high on their agenda too. Schools and colleges where mindfulness has been made part of the school culture have done so because some member of the senior management team has 'bought in'. Every champion needs someone to champion them, with enough 'clout' to get you in the room or in a meeting with people who have the authority or the purse strings to commission this.

With your ally, map out how mindfulness can meet the school's values, needs and agenda and help it achieve its goals (see exercise at the end of the chapter). There is a vast evidence base for this (see Resources) to build a case of why mindfulness can help the school/college community thrive. You can also use the case studies in this book. Build a credible case, but remember that this shouldn't be a thesis! You are dealing with busy people so keep it short and succinct – try and capture it on one side of A4. With the help of your ally, present this at a senior leadership or governors' meeting and lead a short practice. Managers will appreciate a few moments of quiet and chance to decompress.

Here are some sector-leading examples of how inspired and engaged leadership has brought about significant changes at a schools cluster and local authority level.

A schools cluster approach

In 2018, both the head and deputy head of Moorland Primary School in East Cardiff attended a Mindfulness for Senior School Leaders course. This had been commissioned by the Central South Consortium. Both reported that they thought mindfulness had made a significant impact on their well-being, personally and professionally. Having experienced the benefits of mindfulness themselves, they wanted school staff to attend a mindfulness course for their own well-being and potentially train to pass mindfulness on to the children. In that way, mindfulness could be embedded in the school ethos and curriculum.

In 2018, the head worked with other heads in the schools cluster to secure funding from the Pupil Development Grant for Looked After Children (PDG-LAC). They were successful in gaining funding through the Central South Schools Consortium to offer mindfulness courses for school staff. Their bid also included funding for training to deliver mindfulness curricula for children. The cluster were able to pool their PDG-LAC funding to promote mindfulness in all seven schools. This was an innovative way of working. Moorland already had one teacher trained in Mindfulness for Key Stage 2 (Paws b) but wanted to increase their capacity to deliver the sessions more widely.

In total, 22 school staff from Moorland attended the course including teachers, TAs and office staff. Over the eight weeks of training, staff learnt how to calm themselves, step back and have perspective on events in their school life, face difficulties and find nourishment in their lives. The end-of-course evaluation showed an average rating of 8.8 out of a maximum score of 10 for how important this course had been for them.

Staff reported that at the end of the course:

> It has helped me to pause, think and then react. I am definitely more calm.

> I can use the skills to understand the children more and perhaps listen to them in a different, more mindful way. When I am working with staff I can see I am a more patient person.

> We as a group have worked well together and appreciate the positivity that has arisen. We have all thought about ways to make our days more mindful.

Following the course and after a period of practice, one additional member of staff trained in Paws b and the school hosted 'The Present' training for local schools in which three members of their staff were trained. In 2019, mindfulness sessions had been delivered to Years 4 and 5 and one Year 3 class (165 children in total). The benefits for the children were notable:

> At the start of Y4 when I got worked up, I did mindfulness and it made me feel calmer and relaxed. Whenever I get worried now, me and my brother just do mindfulness for a couple of minutes.

> (Comment from a learner)

> Pupil X was so distressed at the beginning of the year that he was unable to engage with his own age group at all. Following mindfulness sessions, he has been able to return to his own age group and is now beginning to focus independently on his learning without adult support.

> (Comment from a staff member)

It is evident that mindfulness is making a powerful impact on the Moorland School community. As they move towards the introduction of the New Curriculum for Wales, the embedding of mindfulness throughout the school will enable the school to fulfil a significant amount of the agenda for health and well-being.

Local authority approach

Carmarthenshire's longstanding investment in its most vulnerable learners, in particular looked after children, has seen commendable improvements in achievement that have been highlighted by Welsh Government working groups. At the heart of this success is the commitment to behaviour transformation – changing the philosophy of behaviour management to *relationship* management, recognising that adults dealing with a distressed and deregulated child need the skills to regulate themselves first, and that many pupils need accessible tools for self-regulation and emotional resilience.

The .b Foundations eight-week mindfulness course (see Resources) has been introduced as one of the core elements of CPD for staff in schools throughout Carmarthenshire, alongside Trauma Informed Schools, ACE Awareness, Emotional Coaching and Restorative Practices. The aim has been to enhance both pupil and staff well-being. Over 200 education staff have completed .b Foundations, with some schools already building a critical mass of staff who have experienced mindfulness training. Over 30 teachers and children's services/central staff have trained to teach .b or Paws b. This includes primary, secondary, the pupil referral unit (PRU) and staff working with a wide range of additional needs.

Schools are at the beginning of their journey in introducing mindfulness to pupils. After an initial lead by the looked after children support team in introducing mindfulness in schools, it is now embedded in the local authority's transformational vision for all schools. Mindfulness is being promoted as a universal offer to both staff and pupils across the local authority. All staff have access to the eight-week .b Foundations course, as well as the newly developed bespoke Mindfulness for Education Leaders, and training for school staff to teach .b or Paws b. In time, it is intended to offer training to teach The Present for 3–14-year-olds.

Jo Antoniazzi (Lead for Positive Behaviour) and Bethan James (Lead for Corporate Parenting) are monitoring and tracking how schools are rolling out mindfulness from the point of view of both staff and pupils' well-being, and will be using the range of data available to the authority to continue to evaluate the impact as part of the Behaviour and Well-being Transformation drive.

Mindfulness and the introduction of some of the underpinning neuroscience provides a shared understanding and language to enable pupils and staff to review and discuss relationships and behaviour and their implications. This far-reaching training programme with mindfulness at its heart has the potential to achieve genuine transformation in the learning environment in schools throughout Carmarthenshire. Schools will also be equipped to deliver mindfulness to pupils as part of the Health and Well-being Area of Learning Experience, getting a head start in establishing the new curriculum for Wales, which has well-being at its centre.

Special schools and the PRU have had whole-staff training in the eight-week course and are already reporting fewer internal exclusions and better pupil engagement, less physical restraints and improved attendance. Bethan James and Jo Antoniazzi have described the initial impact and feedback to date as overwhelming. Children have provided moving testimony of mindfulness helping them calm themselves, concentrate better, deal with stress and anxiety, exams and social anxiety, family issues and realise potential.[5]

Why does this matter?

Research by Hudson et al. suggests that energetic leadership is the single most defining factor in choosing and sustaining mindfulness programmes.[6] The ability to see the potential, think ambitiously about what can be achieved and be persistent in the approach of matching mindfulness to existing policies and agenda can transform an education agenda.

It is evident from the case studies above that significant and powerful developments have been achieved that are improving the lives of staff and pupils, some of whom are the most vulnerable in society.

---

5   L. Williams, Mindful Wales toolkit, Mindfulness Wales (2020). Available at: https://mindfulness-wales.org/wp-content/uploads/2020/10/MINDFUL-WALES-TOOLKIT-Nov-2020.pdf.
6   K. G. Hudson, R. Lawton and S. Hugh-Jones, Factors affecting the implementation of a whole school mindfulness program: a qualitative study using the consolidated framework for implementation research, *British Medical Council Health Services Research* 20 (2020): 133.

The tortoise approach

'It is important to manage expectations and to clarify that implementation is a long-term, slow burn: it can take a number of years to establish across a school setting and build capacity.'[7]

Play the long game. Fads come and go in schools, so don't be surprised at an eye-roll here and there when you suggest the idea. By starting small, by doing this and gathering evidence along the way, particularly anecdotal, it will be more sustainable in the long run.

After all – what are we trying to do in a school/college? It's not just about passing exams and getting qualifications, although these are important. It's about growing a whole human being, giving them skills to flourish and thrive in a future that is very uncertain. In time it could include more staff practising and engaging mindfulness, but this will come. So keep a big perspective, as knock-backs are inevitable. Have faith, don't despair and remember your true purpose in doing this.

---

7   Hudson et al., Factors affecting the implementation of a whole school mindfulness program.

Mindfulness exercises to try

Daring to dream

Take a quiet moment for yourself. Make sure you are grounded and comfortable. Tune in to the breathing. Let the breath come and go, resting in its calmness.

Bring to mind what inspires you about your job.

▓ The learners and the progress they make?

▓ The difference you can see in some of the pupils you've taught, how they've grown?

▓ A sense of giving someone a second chance in life?

▓ Your colleagues and the daily commitment they show, which is inspiring?

Nurture these thoughts and images. Notice any sensations, particularly in the heart area.

Now bring to mind what it would be like if the school/college could be a place where:

▓ People were generally kind to each other.

▓ There was a sense of seeing the whole person, staff and student alike, their struggles and their victories.

▓ There was a sense of gratitude for everyone and what they do to help the school/college thrive. Remember that this includes you.

If you find you are getting overwhelmed then that's fine, just return to the stability of the body and breath. Focus on feeling calm and settled.

This might be a heart-opening experience and so dwelling with any sensations in the body, mind and heart, with calm abiding, can be enough.

When you're ready, focus more on the contact points of the body, the feet on floor and bottom on the chair, and externalise your senses once more.

Space to journal what happened

Why this matters

To try and bring into being something new, you will need a vision. This needs to include the depth and breadth of what you think is possible. You need to contact and flesh out the inspiration that seeks to do this work. You need something to return to, to remind you when you hit inevitable obstacles.

Mapping the territory

Following the *daring to dream* exercise, below is a drawing of a river, with its various twists and turns.

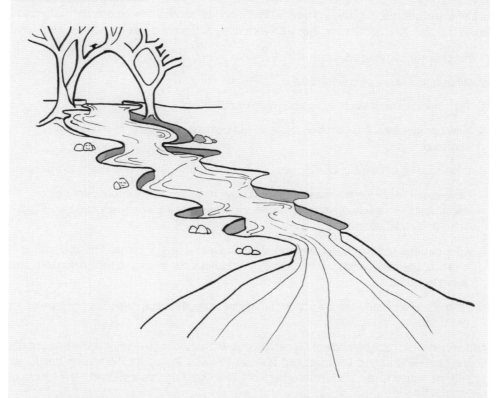

At the start of the river, put where you're at now. For example, what mindfulness experience/training you have done? What resources are available to you?

At the end, write what you would like to happen in your school/college community and why. How would it look?

Now map the steps in between. What needs to happen for this vision to become a reality? Try and be as concrete as possible. When you identify a step, try and write down what's needed for it to happen.

Why this matters

Clarity is the difference between something happening or not. Lots of people have good ideas, but without the clarity of how to take the next step, they rarely come to fruition. This might seem quite simple, but by writing it down, you are making a bridge between dreams and intuition, and action and reality. It will be somewhere to return to when you lose your way. And remember that all rivers eddy and have currents, so enjoy the flow!

In this chapter, we've discussed:

■ What a mindfulness champion is.

■ The importance of keeping up your own mindfulness practice.

■ How competence and confidence are key in being a successful mindfulness champion.

■ Case studies of real-life challenges of champions bringing mindfulness to a school.

■ How senior leadership engagement is crucial in successfully implementing mindfulness in a school. In some cases the vision of senior leaders can be absolutely transformative.

■ Adopting the tortoise approach and not being afraid to start slow. These qualities and attitudes are essential to being a mindfulness champion, to be sustainable and avoid burnout.

■ How it's essential to have a vision but at the same time clarify concrete steps to get there.

And support is crucial – none of us can do this work alone. As it says in the lines of the Shambala (Mindful and Compassion) Warrior Prayer: 'Put down the leaden burden of saving the world alone. Join with others of like mind. Align yourself with the forces of resolution.'[8]

---

8   Akuppa, The Shambala Warrior Mind Training. Available at: https://thebuddhistcentre.com/system/files/groups/files/shambala_warrior_training.pdf

Chapter 12
Mindful Ideas to Try in the Classroom

Once you have established your own mindfulness practice, there are different curricula you can train in to deliver mindfulness in the classroom (information about these can be found in the Resources section). However, once you have practised sufficiently, you may just want to get going and weave a few simple practices into the day. These ideas/ exercises can be used to help settle the class after a noisy lunchtime, or in form tutor time, or to reset the class when energy is flagging. For younger children, they can easily take place in circle time or around afternoon story time. Here are some favourites from teachers and college staff practising mindfulness and bringing it to their classroom.

Early years

This is a wonderful time to introduce mindfulness as young children are so open to new experiences and naturally curious. Lots of early years teaching centres on giving learning experiences with different textures and settings so mindfulness can be easily woven in.

- **The breathing ball:** This exercise involves stopping when the occasion calls for it, either with an individual or group. Ask the children to bring their attention to the breath coming in and out, perhaps putting hands on the belly.

  Model taking at least three long, slow, deep breaths in through the nose, out through the mouth, emphasising a sigh on the exhalation with the children. Using a Hoberman sphere provides a visual representation of the rhythm of inhalation and exhalation as an anchor for the breath.

  > I find it works especially well if a child is upset or energy is scattered. This prac- tice allows me to attune to the child and validate how they may be feeling. It develops their self-awareness of feelings and mood and builds confidence by

equipping the children with a self-regulation strategy that they can use whenever they need to.

(Belle, early years teacher)

- **Tuning in:** Use a chime bar during carpet sessions or circle time to bring focus before teaching. It can also be used to bring closure to the end of a session or relaxation. With eyes open or closed the children listen all the way to the end of the sound. You can let them take turns striking the chime. A rain stick, singing bowl or Tibetan bells can also be used.

  This develops listening skills and sensory awareness of hearing. Listening to the musical notes releases dopamine and appears to positively change the energy in the room.

- **Shake the sillies out:** Dancing, action rhymes and the freeze game can also work. Varying the tempo, fast and slow. Examples include 'Wind the Bobbin Up', 'Heads Shoulders Knees and Toes'. The children find it hilarious when copying going really fast. Always end with a slow version to get their attention back into the present moment before moving on.

  This gets them into their bodies, the physical activity releases serotonin and the endorphins released with laughter release a lot of tension!

- **Kindness:** Giving themselves a big hug, with arms crossing over with right arm on top and then left. Smoothing down both arms and then making a heart shape with hands. Say 'breathing in kindness' while raising the hands up overhead, stretching and opening hands out wide and circling back into a heart.

Primary school

The children might be less 'in the palm of your hand' than when in early years but still open and receptive to new experiences. The following exercises can be used to settle after play time or any time when you feel they need to rest and ground for a few minutes.

- **Tummy and chest breathing:** Place one hand on belly and one hand on chest. Eyes can be open or closed. Feel the rise and the fall of the chest and the belly with the breath. Images can be brought in such as waves on the ocean.

- **Count three breaths (or five or ten):** This is a nice, quick and easy one to settle them, which is accessible, even for the youngest.

- **Bud breathing:** Rest the hands on the lap or the desk. Bring the tips of fingers together like a bud. Then open out the fingers like the petals of a flower in full bloom. This can be synced to the breath, breathing in as the fingers are together and out as they open. Imagery of a flower opening and closing with the sun, day and night can be used. Children often report that this is calming.

- **Sounds:** Tuning in to sounds inside the room/outside the room. Hear them coming and going. Can be emphasised by ringing a chime bar or singing bowl – children are asked to put their hands up when they can't hear it anymore.

Secondary school

Learners are a bit more self-conscious and worried about looking silly in front of their peers. Nevertheless, they enjoy a bit of a break and mindfulness exercises can be helpful when getting frustrated with task, self or others, as well as refocusing.

Finger breathing (in Chapter 1 but copied here for ease)

This is a simple exercise designed to focus and calm. With one finger, trace up one side and down the other of the fingers on the opposite hand. When you have finished, loop back round to start again, or swap hands. Notice the touch between the contact of the fingers. It can be synchronised to the breathing, breathing in as you trace up and out as you trace down. But if this feels too artificial, feel free to let the breath come and go.

Once you've mastered this, you can do it anywhere, like under the desk during a challenging class or meeting. Nobody needs to know you are doing it.

7-11

This is a really useful one for calming down and 'unworrying'. It's particularly effective with anxiety and warding off panic attacks.

- Breath in and as you do count up to 7. Please note that you are not breathing in for 7 seconds but making the count fit the breath. This means you may have to count quite quickly.

- Now breathe out and count up to 11. Again, the count fits with the out breath. The most important thing here is that the out breath is *longer* than the in breath.

- You can use different combinations of numbers like 5–8 *as long as the out breath is longer than the in breath.*

- Why is this? A longer out breath benefits us physiologically by lowering our heart rate and combats fight and flight. This is why you see people blowing out into paper bags when having a panic attacks.

Movement and mindful stretching

As discussed in Chapter 7, not only does the mind affect the body but the body affects the mind. Teenagers are used to skulking and sulking. Gentle, mindful stretching at the beginning or halfway through the class can really release energy and an atmosphere of being stuck.

Sky and earth stretching

Raise one hand up as if to the sky and the other pointing towards the earth. Breathe in and stretch between those two points as if you are stretching every fibre in your being. Breathe out and swap position of hands, i.e. the opposite hand stretches towards the sky and the other hand stretches towards the earth. Repeat a few times.

Finish with either hands on heart or on thighs and take a few breaths to ground.

They'll feel and look better!

Regal posture

From this you can work on posture as they sit back down. Self-consciousness means that many teenagers are round shouldered and tend to stoop at their desks, which isn't good for their mood or their posture long term. Ask them to move slowly back into their seats, noting every movement to get them there. When seated you can talk about 'sitting tall' or 'sitting like a mountain', with the emphasis on a string gently pulling them up from the crown of their head. This will improve engagement and confidence.

College and post-16 setting

Learners have a bit more maturity and can focus for a bit longer. You can use any of the shorter practices you have learnt in this book. For example:

- The mindful minute (see Chapter 2) – perfect for making a transition before or after class or before a presentation, for example.

- Three-step breathing space – a longer practice to settle the group and get them ready for learning.

- Five-minute meditation – start by grounding, asking them to feel hard points of contact with their feet on the floor and body on the chair. Direct the attention to the breath or, if this is difficult for some, to the sensations in the hand. Encourage curiosity and invite them to explore sensations in the hands/the breath. Do the practice yourself and use that as a cue: 'Perhaps your mind has wandered, gently bring it back to the breath/hands.' Remember to leave quiet pauses and not to talk too much.

- Mindful walking outside – spend five minutes slowing down the space and coming into the world of the senses.

- Ask the learners to share something positive that has happened to them in the last week – this really puts them in a good mindset for the session.

  All these practices enable students to be present, improve their concentration and sort out their feelings.

  (Rhianon, FE lecturer)

Final Thoughts

I come from a long line of educators and was brought up in the Rhondda Valley, a mining community that championed education. After years of resistance, I trained as a teacher as I realised that I had the belief that everyone had the potential to learn and develop held deep in my core.

Twenty-five years ago I learnt to meditate and practise mindfulness and honestly do not know how my life would have turned out without it. The values of living a life of awareness, ethical sensitivity, compassion and wisdom have shaped the path so far for me and, in my view, this is the only sane way to live in the world.

As I hinted in the introduction, imagine my joy (and surprise) when these values started to be adopted in a secular form in health, education, workplaces and even the criminal justice system. When I had the chance to train in a programme to bring awareness and kindness into a secondary school setting, I jumped at it. To have the opportunity to express those core beliefs that had shaped my life and bring them into the classroom was powerful. Since then I have had the privilege of training hundreds of school staff in mindfulness practices, and I have recently started to work with school senior management too.

Mindfulness is not a panacea; it won't solve the world's problems. However, it is a capacity that we all have and can cultivate that has been valued through time as promoting the happiness that comes from being authentic. It can help us manage difficulty, be kind and lead a meaningful life based on our values.

There's no denying that the COVID-19 pandemic has made school/college life even more stressful with the shutting down of schools/colleges with the structure and support they give young people, learning how to teach online and in bubbles, worrying about how at-risk families are coping with the isolation. It has taken a toll on everyone in the school community and it is far from over. This is why the well-being of the school community matters most at this time.

When I was a girl I loved superheroes, particularly the Bionic Woman and Wonder Woman. I wanted to be a force for good in the world. Later on, in my Buddhist studies I came across the notion of the Bodhisattva, a superhero/ine who would lead all beings towards enlightenment through their wisdom, energy and deep compassion. I have a painting on my wall by the Welsh artist Kevin Sinnott. It depicts a doctor or nurse in her scrubs, walking up a hill, perhaps on her way home. Below her is a path where

Spider-Man is walking. He looks up at her and waves at her as if acknowledging, 'You're the real hero here'. For me this says it all; super-heroics are not the stuff of comics and films but the everyday actions of people like you. When I was teaching, a school counsellor told me that once a child trusts you, 'You become one of the most important people in their world'. You are the ones reaching out, going above and beyond duty out of genuine kindness and concern, listening when there is no one else to listen, encouraging and empowering all who come into your care. Put simply: you are my heroes and heroines.

I want to help you do what you do best. As we've discussed in this book, compassion needs to be balanced with wise choices, focus with broad attention, self with other, to avoid disillusionment, exhaustion and burnout. Therefore, this book is offered to you as a resource, to help look after yourself, stay empowered and energised, continue to be curious and re-connect with your many strengths. The strength that brought you into the profession in the first place, the strength that enables you to move towards the suffering of others and soften their pains, to champion them and share in their joys and victories, the strength in the knowledge that you have helped shape that human being.

Resources

For your practice

Some people find the structure and commitment of a course helps deepen their practice:

Eight-week mindfulness courses

Online

.begin, a mindfulness course for school staff. The Mindfulness in Schools Project: https://mindfulnessinschools.org/begin-eight-week-mindfulness-course.

Living In The Present, an adult mindfulness course that weaves mindfulness into everyday activity: www.thepresentcourses.org.

In person

b. Foundations, a mindfulness course for school staff. To find a teacher: https://mindfulnessinschools.org/map/foundations-teachers.

Breathworks mindfulness courses, particularly good for those who suffer physical pain too: https://www.breathworks-mindfulness.org.uk.

MBSR/MBCT – the root of all credible mindfulness in education programmes. To find a qualified teacher: https://community.mindfulness-network.org.

Mindful leadership

Mindfulness for Education Leaders (endorsed by the National Academy of Education Leadership): https://www.mindfulnessinaction.co.uk/mel.

Books

Burch, V. and Penman, D. (2013). *Mindfulness for Health: A Practical Guide to Relieving Pain, Reducing Stress and Restoring Well-being*. London: Piatkus.

Kabat-Zinn, J. (1990). *Full Catastrophe Living: Using the Wisdom of the Body and Mind to Ease Stress, Pain, and Illness*. New York: Delta.

Penman, D. (2015). *Mindfulness for Creativity: Adapt and Create in a Frantic World*. London: Piatkus.

Penman, D. and Williams, M. (2011). *Finding Peace in a Frantic World*. London: Piatkus.

Segal, Z., Teasdale, J. and Williams, M. (2013). *Mindfulness-Based Cognitive Therapy for Depression*, 2nd edition. New York: Guildford Press.

Apps (free)

Insight Timer: https://insighttimer.com/en-gb.

Contains lots of different meditations so search for mindfulness. If you don't connect with the teacher you hear, move on. There is plenty of choice!

Going on retreat

The following retreat centres do open retreats that are suitable for beginners. They have comfortable accommodation and good food. They are available for weekend or week-long retreats.

For all: https://www.dhanakosa.com.

For women: https://taraloka.org.uk.

Bringing mindfulness into your workplace

Mindfulness champions training

This gives you the competence and confidence to deliver short practices within your setting: https://www.breathworks-mindfulness.org.uk/pages/events/category/champions-training.

Mindfulness training for the classroom

Early years

The Present – a spiral curriculum for 3–14-year-olds: https://www.thepresent-courses.org.

Dots – mindfulness for 3–6-year-olds: https://mindfulnessinschools.org/teach-dots-3-6/.

Primary school

Paws .b – mindfulness for junior school: https://mindfulnessinschools.org/teach-paws-b/.

The Present – a spiral curriculum for 3–14-year-olds: https://www.thepresent courses.org.

Secondary school

Mindfulness for secondary school: https://mindfulnessinschools.org/teach-dot-b/.

The Present – peer-focused curriculum for secondary schools: https://www.the presentcourses.org.

The evidence base

Baer, R., Crane, C., Miller, E. and Kuyken, W. (2019). Doing no harm in mindfulness-based programs: conceptual issues and empirical findings, *Clinical Psychology Review*. Available at: https://www.sciencedirect.com/science/article/pii/S0272735818301272.

Dunning, D., Griffiths, K., Kuyken, W., Crane, C., Foulkes, L., Parker, J. and Dalgleish, T. (2018). The effects of mindfulness-based interventions on cognition and mental health in children and adolescents – a meta-analysis of randomized controlled trials, *Journal of Child Psychology and Psychiatry*. Available at: https://pubmed.ncbi.nlm.nih.gov/30345511/.

Hwang, Y., Bartlett, B., Greben, M. and Hand, K. (2017). A systematic review of mindfulness interventions for in-service teachers: a tool to enhance teacher well-being and performance, *Teaching and Teacher Education* 64: 26–42. Available at: https://www.sciencedirect.com/science/article/abs/pii/S0742051X17301130?via%3Dihub.

Weare, K. and Bethune, A. (2021). *Implementing Mindfulness in Schools: An Evidence-Based Guide.* Sheffield: The Mindfulness Initiative. Available at: https://www.themindfulnessinitiative.org/implementing-mindfulness-in-schools-an-evidence-based-guide.

Bibliography

Barks, C. (1995). *The Essential Rumi*. New York: HarperCollins.

Burch, V. and Penman, D. (2013). *Mindfulness for Health: A Practical Guide to Relieving Pain, Reducing Stress and Restoring Well-being*. London: Piatkus Press.

Chaskalson, M. (2011). *The Mindful Workplace: Developing Resilient Individuals and Resonant Organisations with MBSR*. Chichester: Wiley-Blackwell.

Chaskalson, M. and Reitz, M. (2018). *Mind Time: How 10 Mindful Minutes Can Enhance Your Work, Health and Happiness.* London: Thorsons.

Davies, J., Hurrell, C., Raynor, P., Ugwadike, P. and Young, H. (2020). A pragmatic study of the impact of a brief mindfulness intervention on prisoners and staff in a Category B prison and men subject to community-based probation supervision, *International Journal of Offender Therapy and Comparative Criminology*. Available at: https://journals.sagepub.com/doi/full/10.1177/0306624X20944664.

Flook, L., Goldberg, S. B., Pinger, L., Bonus, K. and Davidson, R. J. (2013). Mindfulness for teachers: a pilot study to assess effects on stress, burnout, and teaching efficacy, *Mind, Brain, and Education* 7: 182–195.

France, L. (2005). *The Heart as Origami*. London: Parallax Press.

Gilbert, P. (2010). *The Compassionate Mind*. London: Constable.

Gilbert, P. and Marotos, F. (2021). *Compassionate Mind Training Manual*. Derby: University of Derby.

Hanson, R. (2009). *Buddha Brain: The Practical Neuroscience of Happiness, Love and Wisdom*. Oakland: New Harbinger Press.

Hazeley, J. and Morris, J. (2015). *The Ladybird Book of Mindfulness*. London: Michael Joseph.

Hebb, D. O. (1949). *The Organization of Behaviour: A Neuropsychological Theory*. New York: Wiley & Sons Inc.

Hudson, K. G., Lawton, R. and Hugh-Jones, S. (2020). Factors affecting the implementation of a whole school mindfulness program: a qualitative study using the consolidated framework for implementation research, *British Medical Council Health Services Research* 20: 133.

Hwang, Y., Bartlett, B., Greben, M. and Hand, K. (2017). A systematic review of mindfulness interventions for in-service teachers: a tool to enhance teacher well-being and performance, *Teaching and Teacher Education* 64: 26–42.

Kessler, R. C., Berglund, P., Demler, O., Jin. R., Merikangas, K. R. and Walters, E. E. (2005). Lifetime prevalence and age-of-onset distributions of DSM-IV disorders in the national comorbidity survey replication, *Archives of General Psychiatry* 62(6): 593–602. Available at: https://pubmed.ncbi.nlm.nih.gov/15939837/.

Kipling, R. (1976). *A Choice of Kipling's Verse*. London: Faber.

Mental Health Foundation (2020). *Mental Health Statistics: Children and Young People*. London: Mental Health Foundation. Available at: www.mentalhealthfoundation.org.uk.

Mindfulness Initiative, The (2015). Mindful Nation UK report. London. Available at: www.mindfulnessinitiative.org.

Mindfulness Initiative (2016). *Building the Business Case for Mindfulness in the Workplace*. Sheffield: The Mindfulness Initiative. Available at: https://www.themindfulnessinitiative.org/Handlers/Download.ashx?IDMF=46ef10fd-4d64-41f9-91a6-163d52cd304c.

NICE (2022). *Depression in Adults: Treatment and Management*, NICE Guideline [NG222]. London: National Institute for Health and Care Excellence. Available at: https://www.nice.org.uk/guidance/ng222/chapter/Recommendations#preventing-relapse.

Penman, D. (2015). *Mindfulness for Creativity: Adapt and Create in a Frantic World*. London: Piatkus.

Penman, D and Williams, M. (2011). *Finding Peace in a Frantic World*. London: Piatkus.

Petty, G. (2006). *Evidence-Based Teaching: A Practical Guide*. Cheltenham: Nelson Thomas Ltd.

Public Health England (2014). *The Link Between Pupil Health and Wellbeing and Attainment: A Briefing for Head Teachers, Governors and Staff in Education Settings*. London: Public Health England. Available at: https://assets.publishing.service.gov.uk/government/uploads/system/uploads/attachment_data/file/370686/HT_briefing_layoutvFINALvii.pdf.

Rogers, A. (2002). *Teaching Adults*, 3rd edition. Oxford: Oxford University Press.

Rosenberg, M. B. (2001). *Nonviolent Communication: A Language of Compassion*. Encinitas: Puddledancer Press.

Sartre, J. P. (2000). *Huis Clos and Other Plays*. London: Penguin Classics.

Segal, Z., Teasdale, J. and Williams, M. (2013). *Mindfulness-Based Cognitive Therapy for Depression*, 2nd edition. New York: Guilford Press.

Siegel, D. J. (2020). *The Developing Mind*, 3rd edition. New York: Guilford Press.

Silverton, S. (2020). *Living in the Present: Teaching Notes*. Conwy: The Present CIC.

Speck, D. (2019). One in seven NQTs drop out in first year, *TES* (19 September). Available at: https://www.tes.com/news/one-seven-nqts-drop-out-first-year.

Verplanken, B. and Wood, W. (2006). Interventions to break and create consumer habits, *Journal of Public Policy and Marketing* 25(1): 90–130. Available at: https://journals.sagepub.com/doi/10.1509/jppm.25.1.90.

Wax, R. (2012). What's so funny about mental illness? *TED Talks*. Available at: https://www.ted.com/talks/ruby_wax_what_s_so_funny_about_mental_illness?language=en.

Weare, K. and Bethune, A. (2021). *Implementing Mindfulness in Schools: An Evidence-Based Guide*. Sheffield: The Mindfulness Initiative. Available at: https://www.themindfulnessinitiative.org/implementing-mindfulness-in-schools-an-evidence-based-guide.

Williams, L. (2020). Mindful Wales toolkit, Mindfulness Wales. Available at: https://mindfulness-wales.org/wp-content/uploads/2020/10/MINDFUL-WALES-TOOLKIT-Nov-2020.pdf.

Kabat-Zinn, J. (1990). *Full Catastrophe Living: Using the Wisdom of the Body and Mind to Ease Stress, Pain, and Illness*. New York: Delta.

Zerbe, L. (2009). Meditate like a Marine to pump up your mental muscles, *Signs of the Times* (14 March). Available at: https://www.sott.netarticle/256955-Meditate-like-a-Marine-to-pump-up-your-mental-muscles.

About the author

Kamalagita Hughes has been practising mindfulness for 25 years and teaching it for 15. She is a qualified teacher and lecturer with substantial experience in the classroom and in teacher training, further education and higher education. She is passionate about mindfulness as a tool for transformation in the school/college community and works extensively with school clusters, heads, teachers and students to achieve this. She is the education lead for Mindfulness in Action and a lead trainer for the Mindfulness in Schools Project (MiSP) as well as being the chair of Cardiff Buddhist Centre. Kamalagita enjoys wild swimming and lives in Cardiff with her husband and son, and her dog, Tessa.

www.mindfulnessinaction.co.uk/education

@kamalagita @MindfulCardiff

kamalagita@googlemail.com

linkedin.com/in/joanna-blomfield-kamalagita-86816324